THE ARTICULATE
EXECUTIVE

THE ARTICULATE EXECUTIVE

Learn to Look, Act, and Sound Like a Leader

GRANVILLE N. TOOGOOD

McGraw-Hill

New York   San Francisco   Washington, D.C.   Auckland   Bogotá
Caracas   Lisbon   London   Madrid   Mexico City   Milan
Montreal   New Delhi   San Juan   Singapore
Sydney   Tokyo   Toronto

Library of Congress Cataloging-in-Publication Data

Toogood, Granville.
    The articulate executive : learn to look, act, and sound like a
  leader / Granville Toogood.
      p.   cm.
  Includes index.
  ISBN 0-07-065090-X (HC)   ISBN 0-07-065338-0 (PBK)
    1. Business communication.   2. Business presentations.
  3. Public speaking.   4. Communication in management.
  I. Title.
  HF5718.T66   1995
  658.4'5—dc20   95-18292
                                          CIP

McGraw-Hill

A Division of The McGraw·Hill Companies

2 3 4 5 6 7 8 9 0 DOC/DOC 9 0 0 9 8 7 6 5 (HC)
  4 5 6 7 8 9 0 DOC/DOC 9 0 2 1 0 9 8 (PBK)

ISBN 0-07-065090-X (HC)
ISBN 0-07-065338-0 (PBK)

*The sponsoring editor for this book was Betsy N. Brown, the editing supervisor
was Paul R. Sobel, and the production supervisor was Donald F. Schmidt. It
was set in New Caledonia by North Market Street Graphics.*

Printed and bound by R. R. Donnelley & Sons Company.

McGraw-Hill books are available at special quantity discounts to use as premiums and sales promotions, or for use in corporate training programs. For
more information, please write to the Director of Special Sales, McGraw-
Hill, Inc., 11 West 19th Street, New York, NY 10011. Or contact your local
bookstore.

 This book is printed on recycled, acid-free paper containing a
minimum of 50% recycled, de-inked fiber.

For Pat, for Heather, and for Chase

CONTENTS

PART 3. DELIVERY

A WORD IN ADVANCE

The original "City Slickers" movie starring Billy Crystal and Jack Palance had Jack, the last of the old cowboys, and Billy, playing a dude ranch guest, riding off on their horses together. Suddenly Jack, as Curly, sticks his finger up in the air and says something like, "The secret of life is just one thing!" A skeptical Billy replies: "Oh, and what might that be?" and Curly says, "That's for you to find out!"

That little scene struck me, because if there is one thing I have learned in my business over the years it is this one thing: Just five minutes in front of the right audience can be worth more than a whole year behind your desk.

That's why we owe it to ourselves to understand the impact of all kinds of communications in our businesses—because today more and more often our business *is* communications. So why settle for less than enhanced profitability, measurable efficiencies, more effective strategic planning and added value when we speak to people—any more than when we perform our jobs?

What I am saying is that the formula for success is not necessarily all competence. The formula for success, as we will see shortly, is part competence and the rest the ability to *articulate* that competence—in a way that is not *average* or even *predictable*.

Excellence in communication should be as routine as excellence in business performance.

That's why personal communications training is, for most of my clients, just another business expense. Anyone who understands the changes sweeping the world, recognizes that trying to cope with those changes with anemic or nonexistent communications skills, is like trying to run a road race in cement shoes.

Think of what's happening: Restructuring, downsizing, process reengineering, total quality, best practices, economic value added, partnering, integrated diversity, continuous improvement, speed, benchmarking, de-layering, just-in-time inventory, cross-functional teamwork, empowerment, boundarylessness, common vision, entrepreneurism, and globalization.

Audiences include: Employees, shareholders, peers, team members, new business prospects, congregations, conventions, boards, meetings, symposia, academia, panels, and partners.

The dizzying corporate revolution of the 1990s will affect almost everyone alive today—and their children, and children's children. No one can predict if the revolution will ever end, fed as it is by a new standard of constant change.

To deal with change, you've got to communicate—and to communicate, you've got to *think*.

It almost goes without saying that if you want to speak crisply and intelligently—and who doesn't—first, you've got to have something to say. Not only something to say, but in fact if you're smart—and who doesn't want to be smart?—you've got to have *a whole new architecture*.

That's what this book is about. You can call it a technology if you like, but I prefer to call it a whole new *architecture*—to help you quickly plan and think your way with ease and confidence through any communication—no matter how challenging.

Of course, this book also tries to unravel the mysterious, sometimes bewildering business of public speaking. But more importantly, it explores all that happens even before we open our mouths—the very guts of our thinking process, the flesh and bones of our mind's work.

This book is about productivity. About saving time. About being a better communicator. About planning for results and getting them. About new comprehension and surprising performance. About a part of everybody's life—daily communications—that affects every other part.

It's about realizing a part of you that you may not have known was even there, and about reaching a potential you may not have imagined.

When people call me, it's usually to help them speak. But in fact, I actually wind up also helping them *think*. In a sense, I help them design, build, furnish, and decorate an entire house.

How we construct this "house" determines to a large extent how other people see us.

The moment we open our mouths we begin to reveal our "house" and everything in it. The irony lies in the fact that most people don't realize we carry this "house" around with us everywhere we go.

Most of us suffer from this forgivable naiveté.

Yet throughout our lives, people form an opinion of us—almost from the moment we learn to speak. So it is in all of our interests to discover the house and all that comes with it.

Everything you read in this book is intended to provide ammunition against the tyranny of terrrible talk that permeates every level of our corporate and civic lives. Those who master the speaking game will always have a much better shot at winning the battle of ascendancy.

To that end, you can expect to get from this book simple, straightforward, and easy ways to make any speaking assignment more successful. Even though I am a consultant to major corporations, and many of the examples in this book are aimed at the business person, these new techniques are easy to use and remarkably effective for anyone who does public speaking and makes presentations. These include: Politicians, government bureaucrats, community activists, volunteers, fund-raisers, church speakers, or members of any social or civil organization.

You should be able to spend less time planning, have more productive time talking, and know that your audience will get your message right the first time, every time. More than that, people will not only hear what you're saying, but actually leave the room and do what you want them to do.

I am talking about a brand new way of looking at how you think and how you say what you are thinking.

What, after all, does presentation mean? It means *present* information to people who want to be informed. It means seeing trends and changes and vital signs, then talking about them in such a way that people hear and remember what you say, and can take appropriate action, if necessary. Anything less would be a waste of time for speaker and listener alike.

Tiny Tim, the uke-playing media darling in the 1970s, once said that you are what you eat. I would like to add to Tiny's wisdom by suggesting that *you are what you say. You define your place in society by how you talk.* We gain or lose status based on what we say and how we say it.

Yet, we live in a world where our abilities to talk intelligently to one another seem to be declining. In a sense, we have almost decided to let our machines do our talking for us. Computers talk to us and to themselves. Faxes talk to faxes and where earlier in this century we used to talk, now we watch TV.

Today, people who can speak on their feet, be crisp in meetings, or just engage in good conversation have a clear advantage. People in business and politics who can best promote their ideas also best promote themselves—whether they acutally intend to or not. For what good does it do us to be good managers, competent engineers, smart lawyers, and productive workers of any kind if we are unable to express ourselves in our own language?

I predict that technology will never take the place of plain conversation—whether that conversation is two people talking, a group of people meeting, or just one person talking to hundreds, or maybe even millions of others.

People see the *articulate* voice as the voice of reason and wisdom. He who talks well will more than likely do well. He who has good ideas and talks well will lead.

Wonderful things happen when people talk face to face. Deals are made. Decisions are made. Obstacles are cast aside. Whatever the job, the job gets done face to face.

A phone call can be more compelling than a letter, and a face to face meeting is always more compelling than a phone call—provided, in both cases, that you know how to marshal your thoughts and speak intelligently. Business leaders meeting face to face can cut a transaction in two minutes, where the same transaction might take a committee two years. I once shared an elevator with two CEOs of chemical companies who hadn't seen each other for a number of years. By the time they reached the 30th floor, they had agreed in principle to merge their corporations. Statesmen meet and things happen. History takes a sharp turn.

Things happen.

Read on.

Granville N. Toogood

ACKNOWLEDGMENTS

My sincere thanks to Bryan Mattimore, Jacques de Spoelberch, Jerry Gross, and Betsy Brown for their tireless editing contributions, and to Simon Johnson and John Oppanshaw of Stage Screen Productions for their help preparing visual aids graphics. Also to Fran Williams, who suffered through endless hours of typing and retyping, and my friend and associate, James Humes, for his uncommon wisdom, piercing intelligence, and unfailing sense of humor.

EVERYTHING YOU WILL EVER HAVE TO KNOW ABOUT PUBLIC SPEAKING

- The 18-minute wall—and how to get over it.
- The Four As—how to orchestrate your thoughts.
- 10 important writing—and speaking—rules to live by.
- The 8-second drill—the secret to capturing any audience.
- Reversing the wave—starting with the end.
- Projecting into the future.
- The POWER formula—all you will ever have to know about making an excellent presentation.
- How to begin and end.
- The "Rocket"—how to make your presentation really fly.
- The secret of translation—the real heart of your presentation.
- The "necklace"—a simple, yet elegant design of any presentation.
- The most common rhetorical mistakes.
- Six key errors *never* to make.
- The Menagerie of Mistakes.
- Reading a speech *without* appearing to read.
- Mastering the art of Q&A.

PART ONE

THE SPEAKING GAME

CHAPTER
ONE

THE SPEAKING
GAME

"I'm not a good public speaker . . ."
"I'm fine with small groups, but . . ."
"I get so nervous it affects my performance . . ."
"When I stand up to speak, I just draw a blank . . ."
"I hate to speak . . ."

I've heard every objection.

I've had clients who would rather have a root canal than speak—even to a small group. I've had clients whose personalities change so much when they speak, you would never know they were the same people. I've had clients who became so sick to their stomachs that they could not function (one actually had to leave the stage for several minutes). I've had clients who go into a kind of shock and seem to forget for just a moment who they are, what they're doing, and what they are supposed to say. I've even heard of at least one person who stepped up to a lectern, only to drop dead of a heart attack.

This is all part of life—and death—I suppose, but it doesn't have to be. Most people who view the act of public speaking as a bad thing that's to be avoided at all costs are amazed to find that speaking can actually be fun—and well worth the time and effort.

Without question, most people think public speaking is more of an obstacle than an opportunity, more of a problem than a solution. But in fact, the exact reverse is true. There is no single greater opportunity for productivity, profit, and reward than the simple act of opening your mouth to tell your own story.

Yet this is an opportunity that escapes 9 out of 10 people with responsible jobs in America. The reasons, I think are obvious:

1 We are not living in times that place high value on articulation—yet, ironically most people seem to be attracted to and to admire the articulate when they hear it.

2 Most people don't have a clue how to marshal their thoughts powerfully, then present their case most effectively.

3 Most people live under the illusion that if they just perform their job description competently, all will be well. The wholesale axing of hundreds of thousands of largely capable, perhaps even talented, white-collar managers in the 1980s and 1990s put an end to that dangerous misconception.

My own experience tells me that a large number of the managers who remain distinguish themselves with one outstanding characteristic: They are better communicators than their fallen associates.

Today, more than ever before, we see an urgent need for better personal interaction in business. At the multinational level, good communications are not only important but absolutely essential to the successful conclusion of sometimes complex and sensitive transactions. Junior and senior people alike have got to be able to carry the ball anytime, anywhere, and in any situation, no matter how challenging.

GRACE UNDER PRESSURE

One of my clients, whose name happens to be Grace, found herself unable to land in Bangkok because of violent monsoon weather. She'd been sent from New York by her firm to make a presentation to civic and business leaders in Thailand for a contract worth tens of millions of dollars. By the time her plane landed two days late, other firms had made their pitches. The Thai officials had pretty much made up their minds and were reluctant to see her. Finally, a committee agreed to meet with her, for 20 minutes only, in a hotel lobby.

Any hope of a proper presentation went out the window. She knew she had to abandon her original game plan. Forget the expensive slides. Forget the carefully groomed script. Now it was quick thinking, mental discipline, rapid regrouping and reorganization, streamlining, editing, refining. Everything had come down to just a few minutes face to face with a bunch of complete strangers.

All this with a case of jet lag that made her feel like she'd been up for two days—and she had, almost. She felt oddly tipsy, a little punchy. But the stakes were too high to yield to sloppy thinking. The company's immediate future and her career, she knew, hung in the balance.

She cleared her head. She forced herself to focus.

When the Thai leaders arrived in the lobby, they were courteous but refused to sit down. They let her know that they were in a hurry and that the meeting would have to take place standing. To press the point, they glanced at their watches.

It was all over in 15 minutes (originally, she had planned to speak for an hour or more). When they were gone, she sank into a lobby chair and worried that it had gone badly.

The following day she flew home—but not before learning to her surprise and delight that she had won the account, over seven other vendors!

To this day, she attributes the secret of her success to some of the things you will be reading in this book—things that can make it possible for even the most unlikely candidate for a public speaking course to play the speaking game like a pro.

Today, not knowing how to play the game is simply too large a liability. I read somewhere that more than half of all job applicants are turned down on the basis of verbal communications skills judged to be less than adequate. If all these people hit a wall—and probably never know the real reason why—it's mind-boggling to imagine how much wasted effort is being poured into presentations that fail for the same reason.

What if more than half of all the pitches, presentations, speeches, lectures, and assorted other communications all over the world also failed because of poor communications?

What if the number were only half of that?

We're still talking about lost productivity and lost opportunity on a staggering scale. *Anyone who is serious about his career or his company has got to know how to play the game.*

A friend of mine in a mid-size company got an assignment to give a new-business presentation but waited until the last minute to prepare the big pitch. He cannibalized other presentations, made hasty notes, threw together a mixed bag of handouts and visual aids, then rushed to the airport to catch a plane to the prospective client's headquarters in another city.

Not surprisingly, the presentation did not go as well as he might have hoped. The order went to a competitor—a loss of more than $65 million in new business.

When I hear stories like that, it seems only fair to ask, what is the nature of true productivity? Is it more productive to apply oneself diligently every day at one's desk with the aggregate long-term rewards of that labor almost impossible to measure? Or is it more productive to set aside more time—perhaps a day or two—to adequately plan, prepare, and practice for a presentation that could be worth more to your company in just one day than all the fruits of an entire lifetime of bureaucratic diligence?

Why should we not expect higher quality, speed, and productivity from our communications abilities—just as we routinely expect these things in our businesses? Most of us spend our working lives unaware that *we* are in fact the message—that how others see us can determine the degree of our success.

SEIZING OPPORTUNITY

To look, sound, and act more like a leader or someone worth listening to, you've got to begin with right thinking, with a correct attitude. Polls tell us that public speaking for some people can actually be scarier than death. Whether you believe that, it is still important to take the opposite view. Think of speaking as an opportunity rather than a necessary but unpleasant job that has to be done. Think of speaking as fun. Think of speaking as a kind of challenging game or sport, like any other game or sport—a challenge, not unlike golf or tennis, that involves (1) a knowledge of how to play the game; (2) learned skills; (3) good timing; (4) correct moves; and (5) yes, practice and discipline. Think of yourself as worthy, admirable, capable, and not in the least bit shy about grabbing opportunity to secure the success in life you desire (because you know no one else is going to do it for you).

When I talk about opportunity, I mean opportunity in two ways. I mean the opportunity of gaining the advantage in any business relationship, negotiation, transaction, or speaking assignment. We know that the articulate, well-organized, thoughtful, and forceful player will fare better. But I'm also talking about actively seeking opportunities to practice your new skills learned in this book.

That means start by seeking low-risk audiences to hone your skills. Each day some 80,000 people speak on any number of different subjects across the United States. They speak in libraries, community centers, clubs, hotels, motels, churches, and other places where people assemble. Typically, they speak for no compensation or at the most perhaps a small honorarium and basic expenses. They talk on whatever they know: photography, orchids, computer programming, cooking, solar energy, the paranormal.

Once you have learned the basics of speaking from this book, it might not hurt to join a platform organization like Toastmasters International—regardless of whether you have further opportunity to speak on the job. The more practice the better. Toastmasters and others can give you an opportunity to practice, plus find low-risk speaking engagements where you not only can learn the game but can learn to have fun playing it (and afford to make a few mistakes).

Once you learn to command the room and influence the audience, you won't have any trouble convincing yourself that your new sport really is a thrill. One success breeds another—and genuine applause to a speaker is like a tonic that lifts the soul. You may not hear applause in a sales or new business presentation, but you will know and sense when you have done a good job.

HOW TO COME ACROSS AS A LEADER

Lee Iacocca pulled Chrysler back from near ashes and drove it into preeminence. He had it.

John Sculley built Apple into a world power that challenged IBM. He had it.

Jack Welch made GE the model of the early-twenty-first-century corporation. He had it.

Norman Schwarzkopf leaped out of nowhere like a flaming sword of justice to humble Saddam Hussein in Desert Storm and then dazzled the world with press briefings that brought a new element of humanity, wisdom, and restraint to the public perception of war. He had it.

All four brought more than just competence to their jobs. All four shared three characteristics which combine to create what I term *supercompetence*. Call those characteristics the *three Cs:*

1. *Competence* You have to be at least fairly good at what you do. If you're not, plenty of other people would be happy to take your place. More than that, you also have to have a few extra skills handy: computer skills, for example, and maybe a working knowledge of marketing and financial services.

2. *Clarity*   You've got to be able to see beyond the job. You've got to have a feel for what's going on in your industry, have some historical perspective and a knowledgeable overview, understand trends, and be able to project fairly accurately into the future. You've got to be of the mind that change is not only inevitable but, more often than not, actually desirable. Your willingness to embrace change, to trash things if necessary and even start all over again, is your future hedge against your competition.

Your belief that you know where you ought to be going, we will call *having a vision*. You don't have to be a senior person to have a vision, but you can be sure that sooner or later you will attract the attention of senior people.

3. *Communication*   This is the element most often lacking in the equation—the element that says you've got to be able to share your knowledge and information (perhaps even your vision) with other people. It's not in any job description, but you've got to be a translator (explaining the law or technology to neophytes, for example), a teacher, and eventually a leader. The only way you can ever be a leader is to learn to speak effectively.

Lee Iacocca was arguably the finest "car man" of his time. He knew the industry from bottom to top, from design to engineering to manufacturing to sales to market—having spent his entire working life in the car business. He understood the need for change, and he led Chrysler from clunkers to classy quality in a forced march that lasted 10 years. He never faltered in his vision that Chrysler could someday outperform Ford and GM.

Finally, he did it all by using one of his most powerful tools— his formidable ability to persuade and inspire. First, he talked Congress into a huge loan that he paid off 2 years later—with interest. Then he raised the bar at Chrysler in from-the-heart coaching sessions that got everybody up for the challenges ahead. Then he went on TV and told America, "If you can find a better car for the price, buy it!" Millions bought Chrysler cars.

Competence. Clarity. Communication.

John Sculley, fresh from Pepsi, immersed himself deeply in the strange world of Silicon Valley—so much so that he eventually made himself chief of all Apple engineering. Under his guidance, Apple became a big-time "player," not only in hardware but in software, too, posing a real threat to IBM and Compaq, among others. Sculley recognized the need for change and led the company into an expensive but successful marketing blitz. Until he left the company in 1993, he held to his vision that Apple could lead the way into the next century. Along the way, he became one of the most visible executives in America, promoting Apple to every audience that would listen to his views on the future and technology.

Competence. Clarity. Communication.

Jack Welch is the model of competence, clarity, and communication. His story is so well told we need not go into it in detail. It's enough to say that Welch inherited an asthmatic and anemic business in the early 1980s. Ten years later he had turned GE into a world class sprinter and champion long-distance runner combination. Welch was a decade ahead of his time. Change at GE was sweeping and complete. Welch understood exactly what had to be done, and he brought his message to his employees, Wall Street, and customers with passion and depth of vision that rocked every audience he spoke to.

Competence. Clarity. Communication.

Norman Schwarzkopf was a decorated field commander in Vietnam and an Army legend by the time he was named to head Allied forces in Desert Storm. He was an Army career man all the way. He believed deeply in honor, duty, and country, but he was also a man of uncommon compassion and wisdom who lived for his troops. The Army knew him as a great communicator who could inspire men and women to do great things, but it took Desert Storm to show the world the characteristics of grace under pressure, humor, and steely determination that made most of us back home in the States stay glued to our TVs and proud to be American.

Competence. Clarity. Communication.

THE NEGLECTED C

My point is that you can't have competence and clarity without the vital third element—communication. It never did anyone any good to be very able to recognize a problem and to have a clear idea of how to fix that problem if that same person couldn't communicate.

If you want things to happen, you've got to start talking. Those who talk well thrive. Those who talk best lead.

Supercompetence. Good leadership is what the future of American business is all about, and you can't have leadership without supercompetence.

But you don't have to be a leader to be supercompetent.

Supercompetence is the added value that good communications skills contribute in marketable job skills and a healthy, forward-looking attitude. The combination can be compelling and typically manifests itself as advancement up through the ranks of any organization.

Supercompetence is the next logical step for anyone who is thinking about how to get ahead. You've got to know what you're doing, and do it well; you've got to be willing to embrace change; and you've got to be able to acquit yourself intelligently, face-to-face with other people.

And the reality is fairly clear: In the future, supercompetence will be a necessity, not an option.

Here's why: Huge economic and social forces are changing our world. Large components of this ongoing revolution are the sweeping advances in communications technology—the much-hyped information superhighway, the ever-quickening race for the world's fastest PC chips and supercomputers, and the incredible new science of virtual reality that has captured the imagination of most people over the age of three.

THE UNHERALDED REVOLUTION

But there's another communications revolution that's in no job description and not mentioned in the newspapers. This is a revolution that most people who have to work for a living must deal with—in most cases, without help and without proper preparation.

This is how it works. Once (not too long ago) the rules were simple: the boss dictated to the troops, and that was pretty much it. But now, while the boss still talks to the troops—saying here's where we're going, you figure out how to get there (that's empowerment)—now it's a lot more of the troops talking to the troops, working together across onetime boundaries (that's cross-functional teamwork). It's also millions of sales, marketing, and customer service people talking to clients and customers. It's everybody talking to everybody else—to customers, employees, peers, team groups, classrooms, committees, panels, analysts, associates, boards, industry groups, associations, civic groups, congregations, and lots of other vital audiences.

All of which means that the role of management is changing fast. Today managers are expected to lead. You can't hide in your office any more and hope that all goes well, that the thing will somehow run itself. Now you've got to roll up your sleeves, get out of the corner office and the executive suite, and down on the floor. You've got to show leadership. You've got to become a coach and a facilitator. You've got to encourage risk taking. You've got to be seen and heard. You've got to recognize change, be willing to take action, to base your actions on what the market is telling you. Then you've got to inspire others to share your vision. All of this requires talking—a lot more talking both up and down within organizations—than most managers are used to.

Your people have got to learn to lead from your example, then spread the vision throughout the ranks. In the end the talking is infectious. You create a culture of open communication. Everybody winds up talking, sharing ideas, challenging, speaking out, building something together. It's as if you tore down all the walls of your company and unleashed ideas and talents you never even knew existed.

It happened with varying degrees of success at Chrysler, GM, GE, GTE, and literally thousands of other companies in the 1990s.

That's what supercompetence is all about. Just one person exercising supercompetence can make things happen and ensure her or his place in whatever the future has to offer. A million people exercising supercompetence can change the future and the world.

LEADERSHIP

The seismic upheavals of the 1980s and 1990s saw POWER pushed down through the ranks like never before, suddenly making leaders out of people who had to scramble to live up to their new roles in a changing world.

Practically overnight they found themselves thrust into the speaking game, often without a clue how to play it. With only role models to fall back on, most quickly figured out that where you find a leader, you will also find the power of persuasion. And where you find persuasion you find someone who can speak with authority.

On the bright side, you've got Winston Churchill, who convinced the Nazis that the invasion of England, a country which was in fact a sitting duck, would inflict too high a toll upon the Wehrmacht and Luftwaffe. You've got Lee Iacocca, who in the early 1980s persuaded tens of thousands of gullible Americans to buy lousy cars, thereby saving Chrysler. You've got the legendary football coach Vince Lombardi, who elevated the rock-bottom Green Bay Packers to world champions by persuading average football players that they could be great.

In the early 1990s, no one understood the hopes and fears and needs of the American people better than Bill Clinton, who marshaled all his powers of persuasion to get elected, then staged town meetings (which best suited his populist style) to stay in touch with his constituencies and cement his support.

On the dark side, you've got Adolph Hitler, Joseph Stalin, Mussolini, and assorted other twisted geniuses who inspired their fellow people to new heights of evil. You've got Charlie Manson, a diabolically talented criminal mind, who inspired ordinary, middle-class American girls to happily commit unspeakable atrocities. And you've got Vladimar Zhirinovsky, who suddenly popped up on a tide of discontent in Russia like a slavic Mad Hatter, raving about dropping nuclear bombs all over the world.

What do these people, both bright and dark, have that we don't have?

For one thing, they have charisma, and, by nature, they are attracted to the spotlight. (Some so much so that they become like moths to the flame and ultimately self-destruct.) This is a God-given asset or liability, depending on how you look at it, and one which we can't do much about.

But more importantly, charismatics *add value* to what they are saying by *taking a position.* They have a *point of view.* They *translate* situations into positions. They *present evidence* to back up their position, then propose *a course of action. They speak simply.* They answer our objections before we can raise them. *They press the case with conviction.* They *believe.*

That's why they are seen as leaders, and are in fact leaders. This is how leaders talk to us. This is what leadership is all about.

And even if you feel you have no charisma—even if you hate to speak—even if you think your subject is too "dry," too "grey," too mechanical, too boring, too whatever—you can still far surpass your expectations and come across as a leader yourself.

UNDERSTANDING YOUR AUDIENCE

Some people believe that if Winston Churchill had not taken to the airways in WW II, Londoners would be speaking German today.

It used to be said of superlawyers Melvin Belli and F. Lee Bailey that they could persuade almost any jury that a guilty person was innocent and an innocent person guilty.

Billy Graham took his crusade to the world and claims that his ministry has forever changed the lives of millions of people.

If you have something to say and say it well, the world will listen.

First you have to understand the people. When you understand the people, you can identify human needs. When you identify human needs, you can appeal to psychology and thus the mind. I'm actually talking here about two minds: First, the conscious mind, which happily swims like a fish all day long in a pool of intellectual activity, and second, the primal mind, which lurks somewhere in the dark recesses far below the surface. The primal mind hearkens back to hunting and caves and flickering firelight and perhaps violent death at an early age.

These are *two separate beings*. Guess which one you want to be talking to?

If you guessed the primal mind, you're right. Because the primal mind governs our greatest hopes and fears, our loves and hates, our very hearts. The primal mind is like a cagey beast sniffing the wind, trying to pick up the scent of blood. The primal mind is also a mother wolf, gently protecting and suckling her cub with great love. The primal mind reacts to the gut. It *senses* things, vaulting over the oblivious intellectual mind to pick up vital clues and signals. It is driven by our most basic needs: sex, shelter, creativity, power, work, love, hope, food, fear, fulfillment. It wants to be recognized, to be reassured. It can be lured open like a rose giving itself to the sun or snap shut like a frightened clam burrowing itself deeper into the mud.

This is the fellow we are dealing with. This fellow doesn't listen to our data, to our arguments, to our appeals. He's not interested in our intellectual aplomb. He doesn't really care if we're smart, or even if we're dumb.

Yet this is the guy, whether we know it or not—or whether we like it or not—who actually makes most of our important decisions for us—and the conscious mind be damned.

This is the guy who acts on *warm feelings* and on *deep dislike*. He's the profoundly unknowable Instinct Man inside each of us.

He's the one who kicks the tire and decides to buy the new car, the one who steps through the door, says "this is it" and decides to buy the new house, the one who shakes the hand and knows right then and there that this is the right person for the new job.

In other words, this is the guy who makes all the important decisions and runs our lives. Once he's made up his mind, there's no going back. He simply says, "this is my decision," retreats back into the murky depths, and alerts the intellectual mind to make a list of ways to justify that decision.

That's why this is the guy we really want to be talking to. And there are only two ways we can get through to him as he sits out there in the audience:

1 Through ourselves (does he like me?)

2 Through direct appeal to the emotions (stories and anecdotes that touch his heart)

The first part can be fairly easy: try to be yourself, try to be and act relaxed, try to talk like you're talking to a friend.

The Instinct Man will probably accept you, at least grudgingly, if you will but do him the simple kindness of not coming across as unprepared, scared to death, or a complete phony.

The second part, ironically, requires the participation of our intellects. This is where we drift into the business of psychology.

You must appeal to whatever issue happens to be presenting itself. And your appeal must be built on a base of simple (read primitive) human need.

For example, you run a blanket factory for a big textile company. Your entire industry is struggling, the company itself is not doing very well, and you know the factory is failing in spite of everything you've been doing to try and stop the slide.

What do you do?

That's exactly the difficult position in which Bob Dale, who later became president of Fieldcrest, found himself in the early 1980s. Long before empowerment became a popular management strategy, Bob followed his gut instincts: He took his case to the workers on the factory floor and let them help figure it out.

He said something like: "We've got problems. We're all in this together. You guys know these machines. You're all good at what you do. I want you to put your heads together and let your brains and your magic and your creativity help get us out of this mess."

The workers had never heard a boss talk to them like that. They went right to work with inspired gusto and shortly came up with a brand new blanket much thicker and softer than anything else on the market at the time. Even the weave and the textiles were new. The new product sold like hotcakes, and the plant and jobs were saved.

But not every story is so upbeat. In the hard world we live in, sometimes we've got to justify pain to the ones who feel it the most.

If you are a boss in a time of downsizing, for instance, you must dampen the flames of fear by talking about job security, consolidation, corporate stability, future opportunity, teamwork, and shared goals to those lucky ones who escape the ax. To those who must go, there's the message of referrals, outplacement services, retirement options, severance packages, and a candid explanation of why this terrible thing had to happen. If your audience sees you as part of the problem, at least they might also see you as a stand-up person with a heart who wasn't afraid to tell the truth to your face.

One of my clients found himself throwing his prepared remarks away after his company had taken over another company in a hostile leveraged buyout. Thousands of people had been let go. The audience was a combination of clashing cultures. The mood was uneasy.

He was supposed to talk about the company's financial health, slide show and all. But instead he told a little story about how his little boy had found him unable to sleep, sitting downstairs in the dark, worrying about having to fire so many people from both companies in the weeks ahead.

It was the first time his son had ever seen him so vulnerable, he said.

The son, confused and worried, put his arm over his father's shoulder and said, "It's all right, dad. It's got to be all right—because I know if it wasn't, you wouldn't do it."

Then the boy told his father why he, too, had been unable to sleep. Just that very day his best friend in fifth grade had been killed after falling out of a third-floor window. The boy talked quietly about his friend and his sense of shock and loss, not yet fully able to comprehend that his friend was gone forever.

The father listened. In the end, the boy said, "He never had a life—at least the people in your company have a life. . . ."

"At that moment," the father told his audience, "I knew I had a message. I didn't feel good about what had to be done, but I was able—at least, emotionally—to put it into proper perspective.

"The message is that we all have a future, those who are with us today—and those who are not. For those of us who stay, the future has never been brighter. For those who have left us, we hope we have been a stepping stone on their journey to even greater opportunity."

And so it went. The story touched everybody in the audience for several reasons: It reached down into their emotions to wake up the Instinct Man, gave them all a sense of solidarity and a kind of kinship, and served as a life experience that they could all identify with and share together. Most important, it said the man doing the talking was a real human being, and it helped defuse some of the lingering anxieties in the wake of the LBO.

TALKING TO INSTINCT MAN

The good speaker is always on the alert for opportunities to appeal to common sense and our deepest needs.

Advertising people understand this principle better than most:

They're not selling soap. They're selling sex.

They're not selling perfume. They're selling love.

They're not selling cars. They're selling excitement.

They're not selling jeans. They're selling adventure.

They're not selling cigarettes. They're selling freedom.

And a corporate person isn't just selling strategic plans, or making budget proposals, or giving quarterly reports. The corporate person is selling confidence, a sense of well-being, good will. In other words, the corporate person is forever selling *himself* or *herself*. And to enlist the support of listeners, the corporate person has to try to know their most basic needs.

Every member of every audience will silently ask the question, "What's in it for me?" Profit sharing? Safety? Wisdom? A chance for promotion? A way to be recognized? A way to get rich? To find satisfaction? To grow intellectually or spiritually?

Try to answer that question. Then shape the path to your own objectives around the Instinct Man. History is full of people who shaped the paths to their own objectives around the Instinct Man.

PART TWO

ORGANIZATION, WRITING, AND PREPARATION

CHAPTER

FOUR

FIRST STEPS TO ORGANIZING YOUR PRESENTATION

A couple of years ago I got a call from a $6 billion operating arm of a big manufacturing company. They explained that their main competition, a large producer of aircraft engines, was eating their business for breakfast, lunch, and dinner. The market share was roughly 85/15. Something was clearly amiss. Could it be that their new business and client presentations needed work? Would I come and take a look?

I flew out to the client, sat in on a couple of key presentations, and wound up stunned by an apparent paradox: How could such intelligent, competent men and women—top managers, division heads, talented engineers—be so patently inept? I came up with a long laundry list of things I thought might help turn the situation around, got the okay to proceed, and went to work.

For the next several months I met with groups of managers (no more than six at a time to ensure quality) for a total of three days for each group.

I let them witness their own presentations on videotape, then led them through a series of steps to change their thinking, their focus, their procedures, their planning process, their attitudes and objectives, and other categories which needed fixing.

We developed a consistent business message, threw out most of the slides and overheads, shortened the presentations, practiced basic talking skills, redesigned the few remaining visuals, began using anecdotal evidence, introduced a conversational style, got to the point fast, ended strongly, and more.

Then top management sent them all back out into the field.

Eighteen months later, the market share was almost exactly reversed. I do not claim credit for that reversal—though I would like to. The company made a good product. They were able to keep quality while cutting costs, and management made the right moves at the right time. But it did not hurt that roughly three dozen senior engineers who spearheaded the sales and customer service teams were now a lot smarter and a lot more effective in how they presented themselves, their products and services, their company, their profession, and even their industry.

I believe our success in that instance was due, in part, to the fact that we tried to make the presentations easy to understand and remember. Our aim, as always, was simplicity, economy, and focus. But regardless of whether your presentation is elegant and streamlined or fat and burdened with unnecessary numbers and statistics, your first responsibility to your audience is to serve as a *translator*. This is the *added value* that any good presenter brings to the party. Translation is also the engine that propels the rocket (which we will talk more about later), then drives it all the way to its target.

The translator demystifies the esoteric to the lay audience. For example, a speaker explaining the complexities of a merger and acquisitions deal to an audience of, say, civil engineers, would do well to couch everything in simple concept and plain language. The translator should carefully highlight every step, explain why, assume nothing, and monitor progress by constantly asking the question, "Would I be getting this if I were there listening to me?"

Or rather than make a conventional presentation to senior management, an assistant vice president might take a clear point of view based on the data she is presenting and elevate her presentation to a higher level by making specific strategic recommendations—rather than simply present the facts. This tactic by itself would be not only helpful to management, but also cast the presenter as a leader.

IMPORTANT QUESTIONS THAT DETERMINE EFFECTIVENESS

A good speaker, then, must also be able to evaluate, interpret, translate, and project (more on projection later). A good translator is like a good surgeon—excising unwelcome elements with a clear head and steady hand and executing every move precisely and economically.

In a straightforward business presentation, the presenter/translator owes it to the audience, especially if he is reporting up, to come to certain prudent conclusions and even to make recommendations couched as suggestions that probably ought to be considered. This is the essence of information translation and a good indicator of leadership potential for the aspiring manager. Information translation creates order from chaos, gives direction and meaning.

To translate effectively, you have to ask questions:

What does this really mean?

Why is this important?

What should I really be saying here?

What is the point?

Does this add anything?

Am I speaking in a language everyone can understand?

Am I using examples that fit?

Who really cares?

THE FOUR As

Ask questions like these, and the truth will come out. You may be able to see situations and trends you didn't see before. You will force yourself to be crisp, to find the path of least resistance. Every piece of information will tell a small story that is part of a bigger story. It is up to you to orchestrate the essential details, head them all in the same direction, and walk them carefully where they've got to go. Think of it this way:

Assemble—Bring the relevant data together.

Align—Make certain all the facts are headed in the same direction.

Apply—Explain how these facts, put together, tell a story.

Assign—Go the next step and assign added value. That is, take the information and what it is telling you, then project that information into a highly probable future reality. Create a model for the future that will let us make decisions today.

An executive friend of mine complained recently that a management consultant he was considering hiring gave a presentation that seemed not only inane, but pointless. My friend felt suffocated—buried under an avalanche of statistical information presented on slides packed with endless rows of hard-to-read numbers. For three hours he suffered under this onslaught, then confided later that he felt pretty stupid—because he was unable to figure out what the guy was trying to say.

I assured my friend that the problem lay not with him but with the consultant (who, as you might imagine, did not get the job). Either out of ignorance or sheer devious intent, the consultant had "snowed" my friend with enough random facts to ruin a good half-day's productivity, perhaps hoping that the appearance of arcane knowledge would substitute for a lack of competence.

Had he been a good translator, explained in 18 minutes or less (see Chapter 16, "The 18-Minute Wall") how the numbers told a story that could help his would-be client, my guess is that the consultant would have had the job.

So translate and prosper—and watch your clients prosper.

The fact is that most people are turned off by platters of information served up like laundry lists. Once you've ferreted out audience *need,* then you've got to appeal directly to that need through *logic.*

In my own case, for example, I recognize that I am not just in the business of teaching people how to talk better. That is part of it, certainly. But my larger message is better productivity and profitability. I see better communications productivity—whether spoken or written—as a real business need which leads to profitability.

So when I talk to audiences about speaking, and the things you read about in this book, I am really talking about productivity (faster preparation time, far greater presentation effectiveness, consistently higher quality of communications, and measurably better results in every aspect of business from employee motivation to customer satisfaction). No one is against better productivity. So I appeal to logic.

I say things like, what does it profit us to be good managers if employees, customers, and shareholders don't hear what we're trying to tell them? Why are we failing? What do we have to do to turn the situation around? Why should we expect anyone to listen to us? And what do we have to do to make it worth their while? In other words, I try to identify a need that cries out for fixing. Then I logically convince the audience that this need really is as pressing as I think it is. And then I provide what I view as the best possible solution.

A good translator always tries to find opportunities to identify legitimate needs that people may have in any given audience. Once you think you know the need, you may have your message. Once you have your message, you can stand for something. Once you stand for something, you have set yourself apart from the average speaker—even if you may think you are not a particularly good speaker yourself.

For example, David Kearns, the former CEO of Xerox, identified the need for better education. Virtually every business speech he gave focused on that simple theme. He came to be known as the "education CEO." He stood for something, and, no matter what he was talking about, his topic was just another way of saying that we have to beef up our K–12 education process in this country—for the sake of business, for the country and the world.

President Clinton won the 1992 election primarily by identifying a big need, then applying logic to win over his audience and ultimately win the White House. His campaign HQ in Little Rock, Arkansas, had a banner hung in the office to remind everyone what that need was. The banner read, "It's the Economy, Stupid" (a takeoff on the old acronym KISS, "Keep It Simple, Stupid").

Clinton's job was not easy. First he had to explain to the American people exactly what the problem was, then how it got that way, then why it had to be fixed, then how it had to be fixed. With every audience he identified the need, then logically presented his case. By contrast, his opponent, George Bush, was unable to talk about the economy in the same way, because publicly he took the position that the problem didn't exist. Or if it did exist, it would just fix itself and go away.

People will sit still for almost anything—even increased taxes—if you are able to explain satisfactorily the need and logic behind your actions.

So in your own presentations, even if you're giving only a routine quarterly status report, try to stand for something. Try to spot a need, then explain how to satisfy that need. In a business talk, look for changes, trends, or developments. Do these changes present an emerging need? What is the best way to answer these needs and appeal to the audience?

Why are sales off, for example? Could it be the economy—or do we have a problem in productivity, manufacturing, research and development, quality control, distribution, or all the above? Your need is whatever it takes to beat the problem. You take a position when you use the persuasive power of logic to help people see the problem the way you do, then take action to fix it.

You're already beginning to sound like a leader.

CHAPTER

FIVE

DESIGNING THE PERFECT PRESENTATION: THE POWER FORMULA

The most neglected portion of any presentation is typically the preparation, for two reasons: (1) preparation takes time—and busy people often prefer to risk "winging it" than to spend time on something that may not reward them; and (2) they don't have the slightest idea how to put the thing together in the first place—other than some bad habits, like a bad cold, that they may have picked up along the way.

So preparation can be boring and is not always seen to be productive.

But if someone were to offer those busy people a quick, easy way to assemble their thoughts intelligently and allow them to be consistently effective, they would likely invest a little more effort to realize a big payback.

Wouldn't it be nice, for example, if you could follow the same basic blueprint every time and know that your presentations would be half as long but three times as effective?

Wouldn't it also be nice to know that you would never again have to spend two weeks or a month agonizing over the preparation of a big presentation or speech?

Come to think of it, wouldn't it be nice if we could be certain that every audience got our message right the first time, every time, and that they could pass a quiz on what you said when they left the room? Maybe even remember a month or six months later what the message was?

You can enjoy these big paybacks simply by designing your presentation with five key elements in mind:

1 Strong start

2 One theme

3 Good examples

4 Conversational language

5 Strong ending

These are the key building blocks that constitute the perfect presentation. The perfect presentation is a reality and within reach of anyone willing to stretch.

Think of these five elements as an acorn.

Plant that acorn in your head and watch the acorn grow into an oak tree.

That oak tree is a fail-safe technology for busy executives I call the *POWER Formula*. The POWER Formula is like a first-aid kit for your brain. It works wonders and should be with you at all times—especially when you are asked to speak.

CHAPTER
SIX

THE STRONG
BEGINNING

When you begin your speech, you don't have to be funny, and you don't have to be clever. But you should never, ever be boring.

So to make sure you don't get off on the wrong foot with your audience, plunge right in.

The POWER Formula goes like this:

P *stands for Punch.* To galvanize the mind of the audience, you've got to strike quickly. We have already talked briefly about the philosophical need for a strong start. Now here are eight specific ways to begin with a punch:

1. BEGIN WITH THE ENDING. In other words, the conclusion goes first. Start with a strong statement that embraces your message. Omega becomes alpha, alpha omega—the start and finish become one.

This is perhaps the strongest way to begin business presentations, which are typically rated for their clarity and straightforwardness. Nothing could be more clear than an uncompromising statement that says it all. Nothing could be more straightforward than cutting straight to the core within just a matter of seconds. And nothing could make your job of transferring some kind of news to your audience easier than a summary statement that presents the conclusion first.

Getting to the point seems to be a big obstacle in too many presentations. Failing to get quickly to the point does not appeal to the psychology of the otherwise busy people listening, nor does it bode well for the presenter or for the presentation itself. All too often we find that a presentation that seems to lack a clear theme early on, on closer examination actually has no theme at all.

In these poorly designed presentations, a sense of gathering frustration begins to build in the audience. Frustration leads to irritation, and if things don't improve, the audience is left feeling cheated. Think of the hours, weeks, months, even sometimes years of our lives we have given to ineffectual meetings and presentations that we later could remember only as "a waste of time."

You need never waste people's time again if you make it your business to tell them quickly everything they have to know. For example, talking about sales?

Don't say: "It's nice to be here today. In my remarks I would like to discuss the sales outlook and. . . ." How about: "China and India are the keys to our future. Next year we expect the China market to open up completely, and India two years after that. Right now we have only a 2 percent penetration in China and roughly ½ of 1 percent in India, so there's a lot of room for growth. In fact, we expect to capture 30 percent of the market in both countries within 5 years. . . ." That's the bottom line. You just made the bottom line your top line (headline?), and your conclusion your beginning.

At a crossroads in your company?

Instead of, "Today I would like to talk about implementing our strategic plan and review the committee recommendations, then discuss our contractual obligations with our unions and . . ." (Yawn.) Why not say: "Our choice is clear. Either we make big changes starting today, and dominate the industry once again—or we keep on doing what we're doing and run the risk of going out of business in 2 years. . . ."

Too strong? Inappropriate? Maybe—depending on the circumstances. But in my view it is a far, far better thing to get right to the point and run the risk of being identified as a high-potential individual than stay forever a slave to convention and a source of boredom to busy people.

If you are reporting up within your organization and your presentations are viewed as anything other than good, you are doing a disservice to the senior people to whom you are reporting. You are probably also doing yourself a disservice, which could eventually be reflected in your job status or compensation.

If you are reporting down, a mushy message could be seen as an inability to lead.

So to avoid any chance of being accused of obfuscation, begin with a real bang.

The chair of one of the giant companies I work with has the reputation of being extremely impatient, especially when he sets time aside to hear business reviews and presentations. His senior officers have learned through bitter experience to get right to the point. The rule is, tell the big picture in the first 45 seconds, then spend the rest of the time explaining how you come to that conclusion—what I call "reversing the wave" (more on that later).

In one particular case, a corporate vice president who ran a $3 billion operating company was scheduled to make his first quarterly review. He spent days agonizing over the piles of data, preparing dozens of slides, working and reworking his material, adding and subtracting information, changing the text, editing, and generally driving himself crazy.

But when the big day came, his message was garbled in a mountain of data, and he seemed to take forever to get to his point. Afterward the audience spent more time talking about how tedious his presentation was rather than what he actually said. Another key opportunity lost and another presentation that certainly did more harm than good.

2. TELL A PERSONAL STORY THAT MAKES A BUSINESS POINT. This does not mean try to be funny. Telling your own story is certainly one of the most engaging and personal ways to capture the attention of any audience. Say, for example, that you want to make the point that globalization is an essential ingredient for the future success of your company. You might begin (after a pause) this way:

> When I was shopping at Harrod's in London on a recent business trip, I noticed that even though the shelves were filled with merchandise, I wasn't able to find any of our own products—no matter how hard I tried.
>
> By contrast, yesterday I was in Bloomingdale's in New York, and our products filled the display cases of the cosmetics section.
>
> The problem is that in London, people were buying. In New York, Bloomingdale's was practically empty, and the cash registers were silent.
>
> You don't have to be a business school graduate to see that there's a basic economic sea change in progress here. . . .

In this case you are sounding a kind of wake-up call to your audience, drawing their attention to the need for global strategic planning within your organization or perhaps within your industry.

This is the kind of beginning that might work, let's say, for a marketing vice president speaking to a trade association.

3. USE AN ANECDOTE, ILLUSTRATION, OR ANALOGY—NOT A PERSONAL STORY—TO MAKE YOUR BUSINESS POINT. Something you read in the paper, heard on the radio, saw on TV, something somebody told you. For example, if you want to make your point about the need to go global, you might say:

> I read in the paper yesterday that one of every three U.S. companies now gets half its revenues from operations overseas—and that that overseas trend is only expected to continue.
>
> But if you look at our industry, the reverse seems to be true—and that reverse trend can spell trouble for each of us here today. . . .

Again, you are making a case—this time by drawing on the world of information around you to drive home a point.

4. USE A QUOTATION TO START. Borrow from a famous person to establish your business point. You might find this approach inappropriate for certain audiences. Or you might find it personally too cutesy or manipulative. But in the right setting a good quote that actually helps make your point can be just what your presentation needs. For example:

> Thomas Jefferson once said that the great joy of being an American was simply having freedom of choice. . . . Well, I am sure that if Jefferson were alive today he would certainly agree that at no time in our history have we had more chance to choose our future opportunities.
>
> I am talking about the abundance of opportunities that await us—if we recognize that the future success of our business depends almost exclusively upon how well we sell our products overseas. . . .

By borrowing from Jefferson you have added a certain statesmanlike quality to an otherwise straightforward capitalist concept.

5. USE A RHETORICAL QUESTION. This is an old device that works every time. The question is intended to jolt the audience to pay attention right away.

A rhetorical question is a question simply for its own sake. It is what it says—a rhetorical device that need not have a real answer. Its sole reason for existence is to highlight an issue. For example:

> Why is it that every time I meet business people from Asia or Europe, they keep asking me why America has decided to stay out of global markets?
>
> Well, the answer is that America is very much in global markets. The problem is that while we may believe it, it seems that almost no one else in the world does. . . . And why is that? (Pause) Because we still can't compete. . . .

So the speaker is quickly setting up a proposition: We think we are global, but the rest of the world does not. We think we can compete in the international marketplace, but the rest of the world apparently does not. The rest of the speech, if played properly, will dance to one song: Here is the problem as I see it, and here is what I think we ought to do about it.

6. PROJECT INTO THE FUTURE. The world loves a seer, and audiences are no different. Take a flyer and try to make a prudent estimate of things to come: Do you see changes, new situations, different conditions ahead? The most prudent among us might venture to cast their auguring nets only several years out in the event their projections are dead wrong. But some of today's most successful business speakers and authors position themselves as flat-out futurists. They have no problem looking out 50, even 150 or 200 years into the future, where you can be sure they are safe. Surely if you predict events just 20 years down the road, you may be fairly secure in the knowledge that the majority of your listeners won't remember—or care—what you said way back when. (Besides, they might not even be around to have an opinion.)

So go ahead and have a little fun—with the right audience. People love to believe they have had a glimpse into the future, and if you follow your strong lead with credible evidence based on sensible presumptions and current fact, you might even be able to convince yourself that what you see coming will really happen. For example:

> Thirty years from now, the company you work for probably will not exist. Your work week will be just three days. You will work at computer terminals in your home office two of those days, with the third day devoted to meetings with fellow work associates in production centers run by corporate city-states. You will spend another two days energizing and brainstorming in think tanks run like round-the-clock conference centers by corporate city-states. . . .

That's quite a picture you've just painted. Arguable but interesting enough to make me want to hear more. For all you know it might actually come true—because some of these seemingly wild premises may have some foundation in fact, based on what we are already beginning to see.

Going back for a moment to our centerpiece of globalization, it would not be difficult to provide an intelligent link between our dramatic future depiction, and how these great changes could be the eventual result of worldwide political, economic, social, and spiritual shifts we are beginning to feel even now.

You should note, by the way, that people who like to position themselves as leaders, whether in business or politics, are also fond of future projection and don't hesitate to jump right in where others may fear to tread. So feel free. Jump right in with them.

7. LOOK INTO THE PAST. Looking into the past is another way people who see themselves as leaders attempt to justify their stewardship. But I am not talking about looking into the past in the conventional sense. The key here is to define the past to reveal change. Leaders understand change. One reason they are leaders is that they make it their business to identify changes in progress. If you can do that consistently, the world needs you—because people like you can harness history, control it just enough not to get run over by it. With luck people like you can put inevitable change and evolution to good use.

So a leader sees himself as someone who has the big picture, an historical perspective—someone who can command a world view, size things up before they become a problem, take action in advance of need (what some business people call being "proactive"). Corporate CEOs love to see themselves as statesmen, powers not only in their own corporate back yards, but real players on the world stage. I have written many a speech for many a corporate chief that sweeps through 50 or 60 years in just a few seconds—giving the unmistakable message to audiences that here is a person who has his act together. For example:

> In 1970, the Japanese had just 2 percent of the worldwide telecommunications business. But in 1990, the Japanese commanded 42 percent of the telecommunications business around the world. . . .

> If this trend continues, we can expect that by the year 2020 the Japanese will dominate—and we might not even be in the telecommunications business anymore. . . .

That to me is a bad dream that doesn't have to come true. And that's why I'm here today—to send a wake-up call to every senator and representative in Washington. To compete globally with the Japanese we have got to have a level playing field. Right now. Today. . . .

Bingo. Point made, forge ahead, drive hard to the finish, and then finish hard.

8. HUMOR. Humor is very high risk, and I don't recommend it. Even the funniest, most facile speakers sometimes wind up sounding sarcastic, insensitive, snide, or downright dumb when they try to get a laugh. If a joke goes wrong, for any number of different reasons, the unfortunate result is often a weak, pathetic kind of embarrassed tittering that is mostly an awkward expression of sympathy for the hapless speaker. When an early joke goes flat, it tends to take all the bubbles out of whatever follows.

Why do so many people insist on starting a speech with a joke? One, they see others do it, so they think it is the way to go. Two, they simply don't know of any other way to start strongly. And three, they think a joke will "break the ice" (it can, but probably not in the way they intended).

Even when a speaker is smart enough to use humor to make a legitimate business point, there are other mines in the minefield. For example, I heard a speaker recently begin by telling the story of the woman who was sunbathing naked on the roof of her hotel with nothing but a skimpy towel. When the manager came to the roof to protest, the woman argued that there were no other buildings, no helicopters, no way anyone could see her. The manager said, "No, no, madam. You see, the problem is you are lying on the dining room skylight!"

The speaker then immediately went on to make the point that there are two sides to every issue, and proceeded to present the opposing view.

Nice try. Technically, his execution was correct. The story made a point and he told it correctly. But the women in the audience, most of them MBAs, were not amused. Some of them later let him know it, saying that they thought his sense of humor was insensitive and inappropriate. Given the circumstances, they were probably right.

If you insist on trying humor, make certain you abide by these three rules:

1 Tell the story as if it were true. The punch line is a lot funnier if we aren't expecting it.

2 Tell the story to make a business point. If you don't make a point, you have no business telling a joke.

3 Make sure you tell the story correctly, don't mess up the punch line, and make sure it's appropriate.

CHAPTER

SEVEN

FORGING A POWERFUL MESSAGE

O *stands for One theme.* Churchill said that you can't talk about more than one thing at a time. This is particularly true when you are just one of a series of speakers at a meeting or event. It is tough enough to try to remember what everyone said if all six play the game correctly and each one has only one message. You've still got half a dozen concepts to try to digest.

But the reality is always worse. The reality is that each speaker will very likely *not* know how to play the game and will try to cram a lot of information into a very small time space—without thought to what is the larger truth, what is the real message. What I'm saying is that it is never enough to simply catalogue information and present it to your audience on a tray. It is never enough simply to rattle off a laundry list of things you want to say.

This means take a position. See a change or trend or development and present your case from that point of view.

So exactly how do we add value? First, we determine what our real message is. Let us say we have determined that our theme is globalization. When we translate globalization into a simple sentence, we come up with something like: "The future of our company depends in part on our ability to plug into the global economy." Fine. Now we have globalization translated into a business message coupled with a real sense of urgency. That's a big subject full of possibilities and more than enough to talk about in the next 18 minutes or so.

Now you might argue that while it is all right to talk about globalization, you also want to talk about a lot of other things that affect your business.

My answer is that you may certainly discuss all these items, as many as you like—as long as you clearly link every subtopic to the original overriding concept of globalization. So if you must talk about research and development, for example, under the principles of the POWER Formula you could only discuss research and development as it relates directly to globalization. Research and development would then become an aspect of globalization, as would strategic planning, marketing, advertising, and all the rest.

TALKING WITH PICTURES

W *stands for Windows.* In our model, a *window* is a way to see inside the presentation. Windows represent concrete examples.

A strong message without specifics to back it up is a bankrupt message. Every proposition needs proof for credibility. So to provide credibility, we have to build in windows—concrete examples, pertinent illustrations, proper data, anecdotes or analogies that provide the flip side to concept. A concept is only an abstraction, and abstractions are about as easy to remember as a dream after waking. Every idea linked to a theme must have a concrete example, a window, linked to the idea—because we know from experience that ideas which try to stand alone fall alone. They go in one ear and out the other. So it is not a good use of an audience's time to endure a string of abstractions—and the problem is only compounded if subsequent speakers make the same mistake.

Ernest Hemingway said: "Don't tell me about it—show it to me." That's how he wrote. He *showed* you the matador dying in the bloodied sand of the bull ring, then let you see what death was like through the matador's own eyes. Hemingway *showed* you what fear was like as German soldiers stormed stone walls. And that's what you've got to do. You've got to build little word pictures and give solid information.

To say you had a "great year," for example, has no real value, no credibility. Why a great year? How? Compared to what? Measured in what way? On what do you base your claim? The basis for the claim is more interesting than the claim itself, because specific examples are always more interesting.

So tell them about the surprising turnaround in sales in the southeast, for example—up more than 50 percent over last year. Or about the favorable article in *Business Week*, or how your trip to China produced a bonus order of 20 million units for the Chinese market.

Failing to provide your audience with examples is like a lawyer presenting a case in court but forgetting to provide proof. Your "proof" as a speaker are the examples you pull up to prove your case. If our topic is globalization and our subtopics are strategic planning, research and development, quality control, management development, and so on, then we now add another dimension—another level down—which gives weight to the subtopics and is made up exclusively of relevant examples. Put another way, the examples modify the subtopics, and the subtopics modify the theme. We include nothing extra, no tangents, no distractions.

To illustrate further, if you were making a presentation and arrived at the part where you were explaining the vital link between strategic planning and global achievement, you would now want to begin giving interesting examples of what you mean. You might mention, for instance, a case history of a company that executed a certain strategy successfully and came up with interesting results. Conversely, you could talk about another company that failed to have any apparent strategy at all, and got crushed. Or you could offer a "what if"—

present a hypothetical case that paints a positive or negative view to reinforce your point.

> Just remember that it will profit you little to prepare carefully, present eloquently and articulately, and be in complete command of your subject if your audience doesn't get or remember what you said. Too often we believe, wrongly, that just because we understand, other people understand. To really help people not only understand but remember months later, we should shower them with examples.

The bottom line here is that a presentation with no examples, a presentation that sounds more like a white paper or an academic thesis, is no presentation at all.

THE CONVERSATIONAL APPROACH

E *is for Ear,* which means be conversational. The toughest 3 feet of your life can be simply the transition from talking sitting down to talking standing up. Many of us seem to speak differently on our feet than we do sitting down, and for some the difference means a marked slide in effectiveness. The trick is to be consistently conversational sitting down or standing up.

We are always at our best when we are ourselves, speaking conversationally. Whatever barriers exist between you and your audience can vanish when you talk the way you normally talk.

> Stop thinking that every time you stand up to say something you are making a speech—because you're not. What you're really doing is having an enlarged conversation—even though there may be 100 people listening, and even though you may be doing all the talking.

You always have a choice when you enter into a dialogue or communication of any kind. You can clarify. Or you can obfuscate. Sometimes people obfuscate without realizing it. But some people, for lots of different reasons, actually obfuscate on purpose.

The acknowledged master of incomprehensible language is the seasoned bureaucrat—a wily creature who has been known to devote his entire working life to dodging responsibility and remaining almost totally faceless, forgettable, and invisible. All of which requires a considerably developed repertoire of verbal camouflage. An experienced bureaucrat can raise the art of obfuscation to ingeniously ambiguous new heights.

Take, for example, the venerable Alan Greenspan, chairman of the Federal Reserve Board. Greenspan and other Fed chairs before him have had a long tradition of cryptic allusion in public commentary, which allows them to hint at future action without feeling obliged to actually take any action. Here's what Greenspan told Congress: "Our monetary policy strategy must continue to rest on ongoing assessments of the totality of incoming information and appraisals of the probable outcomes and risks associated with alternative policies."

Translation: It's tough to set interest rates.

Greenspan: "When the Federal Reserve tightens reserve market conditions, it is not surprising to see some upward movement in long-term rates as an aspect of the process that counters the imbalances tending to surface in the expressionary phase of the business cycle."

Translation: The Fed's rate hike tanked the bond market because of fears of growth and inflation.

Greenspan: "Our long-run strategy implies that the Federal Reserve must take care not to overstay an accommodative stance as the headwinds abate."

Translation: We'll tighten some more.

The IRS has proved itself consistently capable of taking bureaucratic fog to even more astonishing heights. Memos and reports—like books, newspaper articles, and speeches—

should always be written the way we speak. With that in mind, consider this IRS proposal to improve the agency's security: "Complete validated Security Architecture; develop data encryption strategy and issue encryption Request for Proposal (RFP); pilot External Access Utility (EAU); prototype Audit Collection functionality."

Phew. No wonder millions of Americans can't get a straight answer from the tax collectors in Washington.

With the exception, perhaps, of bureaucrats, language tends to get simpler as you move up the ladder of any organization. In the board room the communication is typically straightforward, unpretentious, economical, and peppered with breezy, everyday clichés, which can arguably be a mistake in writing but serve as a kind of shorthand in speaking.

By contrast, middle managers, who report up to the people who work for the people in the boardroom, sometimes tend to speak in a corporate "secret handshake" language that is intended often to draw more attention to themselves than what they are actually saying. At the middle management level, or what is left of middle management, it is sometimes possible to be lulled into a kind of hypnotic stupor by the manta of swarms of buzz words.

The hidden agenda here is obvious, and only a reminder of the frailties of human nature. When middle managers salt their presentations with the insider language of a particular discipline, what they are really saying is, "Hey, pay attention to me. I've got a good education, a good track record, and a lot of expertise—and I'd like to be appreciated."

So, instead of saying, "We ought to spend more money on this idea in R&D," which is what you'd likely hear in the boardroom, the presentation two levels down might sound something like this: "Vis-à-vis the question of viability, it may be necessary to interface with R&D in terms of measuring the projected relative scope of the product as it applies to the bottom line parameters of future sales, to impact our decision-making process in order to pro-opt a similar strategic move which could conceivably be undertaken by a near competitor. . . ."

This may be a tiny exaggeration to make a point, but I have actually heard and read worse. The irony is that senior managers are always grateful to hear presentations that are stripped of the burdensome language baggage they have to put up with every day. I know because they tell me so. And yet the further irony is that language changes won't be happening in a big way any time soon. The reason is psychological: Most people measure their self-worth by the work they do, and they simply refuse to believe that larding presentations with quasi-intellectual, privileged language can be anything but rewarding. The self-conscious language of the discipline only reinforces a notion of self-importance. It is a crutch, a prop which many people value as much as a well-tailored business suit.

Sadly, nothing could be further from the truth. To some degree, we are all guilty—lawyers, business managers, sales people, marketing whizzes, engineers, teachers, and professors. Rather than prop us up, the language barriers we erect only serve as distractions, leading us away from our objective of clarity until we collapse under the weight of our own words.

Some years back former Chrysler Chairman Lee Iaccoca went to Washington to try to keep his company alive. Chrysler was threatened with bankruptcy, and Iaccoca needed a lot of money fast. In the senate committee room where he was scheduled to present his case, he was accompanied by a battery of lawyers and what looked like a prepared text about 3 inches thick.

The lawyers swarmed around Iaccoca, but he brushed them aside and then shoved the fat text aside, too. He sat down behind the microphones, faced the senators, and said something like:

Gents, the situation is very simple. I've got 100,000 people who could be out of work in Michigan next week. Now, you can write them a check. We call that welfare, and these workers can go on the public dole. The taxpayer—your constituents—can pay for it. . . .

[Pause here—you can be sure he's got their attention.]

Or you can write me that check, and I'll put these people back to work. We'll build the best cars in America, and we'll do it in just three years. Then I will personally pay back the money—with interest. . . .

And you can take that to the bank!

The senators practically threw the money at Iaccoca. A meeting that was scheduled to take half a day was basically over in 20 minutes. Iaccoca got his money, the Chrysler Corporation had a new lease on life, and a lot of people kept their jobs. Never mind that the cars Chrysler built were arguably nowhere near the best in America (that took another 13 years), it was still a good day all around. The government later got its money back on schedule with interest as promised, and everyone came out a winner.

You could argue that the only reason Chrysler exists today—the only reason you can still buy a Jeep Cherokee—is that its chairman had the good sense not to go to Washington sounding like a businessman.

The paradox here is that a businessman should not sound like a businessman. A chemical engineer should not sound like a chemical engineer. A lawyer should certainly not sound like a lawyer—and you can be sure that a consultant like myself should go out of his way not to sound like a consultant. I like to tell people that if I had a Ph.D. in communications, I probably wouldn't want them to know about it.

Why? Because nothing gets in the way of doing business more than language that is anything other than conversational.

Ask anyone in business today, and they will tell you that most real business gets done *outside* the meetings—when we bump into people in the corridors, pick up the phone to bounce an idea back and forth, in snatches of conversation on the way to someplace else. In other words, when we exercise our most consistently effective communications tool—ourselves. And we are only really ourselves when we are talking to people naturally, conversationally.

The real action comes down to face-to-face, whether one-on-one or one-on-many. And that real action we're talking about is an important component of leadership.

THE STRONG FINISH

R *stands for Retention.* *Retention* for our purposes means strong ending. It is as necessary to have a strong ending as it is to have a strong beginning. After all, this is the last thing you will be saying, so it only makes sense to make the last thing memorable. Don't forget that you want your audience not only to remember what you said but to actually go do what you want them to do. So your takeaway has got to be worth taking away.

There are six ways to end strongly:

1. *Summarize your key point or key points.* One or three, but not two or four, because the ear likes the odd number (two anticipates three, and four is too many to remember).

This means that you could restate your main message, then perhaps give three reasons, or subthemes, to back it up. Or just give your main message and forget about the subthemes. If you chose to give two main messages at the end, this would only serve to divide at the very moment you should be unifying and is no more workable at the end than it is in the beginning or the middle. Best rule of thumb: Stick with one big message and leave it at that. For example: "So our future, as you can see, lies in our own hands. It is not too late to correct our mistakes and to recognize that our success will depend on our determination and ability to expand rapidly into the global marketplace."

2. *Loop back to the beginning.*   Let your ending echo your start. This technique is not only intellectually satisfying and in a design sense aesthetically pleasing, but it can also save time in preparation. That's because if you are in a hurry, once you figure out what your theme is, and you can synthesize that theme into simple but assertive language, then your theme can become not only your bottom line (the last words) but also the top line (the headline, the first words). As before, Alpha becomes Omega, and vice versa.

Of course, you can do the same with virtually any of the eight ways to start strongly that we discussed earlier.

So at the end you would reach back to your beginning and pull up the personal story, illustration, strong statement, quotation, rhetorical question, look at the past or future, or any variety thereof as a closer. Naturally, you would want to couch the retelling in different words so it didn't sound like you were memorizing a spiel off a tape in your head.

For example, you might say: "My hope, then, is that if we do our jobs right, I might be able to find on my next visit to London that our products are on the shelves not only at Harrod's, but every other department store, as well . . . and in France and Germany and Italy, and eventually even in Eastern Europe. And I see another day soon when those cash registers will begin to ring again at Bloomingdale's and all over this country, then all over the world—when people are buying (*product X*) from Seattle to Singapore and from New York to New Delhi."

This could be a new CEO with a new worldwide strategic plan talking to his own troops for the first time. By referring back to the Harrod's/Bloomingdale's anecdote, he has reminded everyone that he is a personable kind of guy with a king-sized vision.

3. *Ask the audience to do something you want them to do.*
You can ask for permission to begin a project; ask for money from the board to pay for that project; ask for help, endorsement, ideas, cooperation, authority, consensus, anything. As any good salesperson will tell you, sometimes if you don't ask, you don't get. Sometimes you don't even get the order if you don't ask for it.

A politician will often ask for help, or the vote. An evangelist might present his case (you're going to hell) and then ask for money. A senior corporate officer chairing a meeting of disparate and perhaps competing elements of the same company might demand cooperation and ask for consensus.

4. *Appeal to the positive.*   If a situation is not favorable, seek whatever good news you can and put a good face on an otherwise not encouraging story. As a matter of course, we often overlook the occasional pieces of gold buried in all the gravel we have to deal with every day. For example, if the dollar is weak, tourist travel overseas will be down, but so will our trade deficit, because our products will cost less. If earnings were off again this year, that's bad. But if they were up from what they were last year, that's good. If we project that curve upward into next year and beyond, we could soon be making a lot of money again.

In business as in life itself we can borrow an ancient axiom made popular recently by Jesse Jackson and others, and choose to view setbacks either as obstacles or as stepping stones. We can see a setback as a body blow, or view it as a challenge. We can complain and feel sorry for ourselves and our situation, or we can look forward with anticipation to a challenge

Mistakes, challenges, obstacles, and setbacks all offer opportunities to sharpen skills, focus energies, stir the creative juices, think smarter, act faster, perform better. The same is true for your presentation, not only in the preparation and delivery but also in the message. Leave your audience with a sense of hope, a looking up and ahead at things rather than down and back.

5. *Project.* The real news in most business presentations is not what happened yesterday, or what's happening today, but what we can expect will happen tomorrow. That's the added value our presentation gives to senior corporate officers, who can base their decisions on what their subordinates tell them. Those subordinates, in turn, base their projections on what happened, let's say, in the last couple of quarters. A division vice president provides good service who makes recommendations to the senior management committee on the board based on intelligent projections which themselves are the product of solid data.

So the real news should be what's coming. If a big change in the demographics, say, of the customer base of a large insurance company is unfolding, then senior management will have to know about that change, and take appropriate action. If federal legislation is in the works that would severely restrict or even ban the sale of a given product, then that information has got to take priority in any presentation relative to the endangered product. If the financials or sales and marketing numbers are developing into a pattern over recent quarters, that's important information. You've got to know where those numbers are heading, what the changes mean for the business, and what we ought to be doing about them. Then you've got to project.

You are now *translating* essentially random data into useful information which can have a measurable dollar effect on the company. One reason so many business presentations fail is because they lack the added value of clear translation, mentioned earlier, and intelligent future projection.

I am talking about recognizing trends and changes and vital signs, then ending your talk in such a way that people hear and remember what you say and can take appropriate action, if necessary.

6. *Tell a story that embraces your theme.* This can be difficult, and if not done correctly may hinder more than help—because a story, if told self-consciously or without conviction, can sound precious and manipulative. But if executed skillfully, there is no better way to end.

First of all, if you use a story you must pick one that hits the mark exactly, doesn't take too long to tell, and makes a clear business statement. The story you choose should also be timeless and serve as a kind of fable. For example, if you are making the point that your company must build a first-rate marketing team to compete in the global economy of the future, you could end this way:

> . . . When I think about the job ahead of us, I think of the lone traveler in the Middle Ages who came to a place where three people were working by the side of the road.
>
> The traveler asked the first worker what he was doing, and the first worker said he was shaping rock.
>
> The traveler asked the second worker what he was doing, and the second worker answered that he was building a wall.
>
> Then the traveler asked the third man and the third man explained . . . that he was building a cathedral. [pause]
>
> Well, in a similar sense, while we're not exactly building cathedrals, I think it's fair to say that we're trying to take the longer view—to create something of enduring value that will continue right into the next century.

Now you shut up. Your job is done, and done well. To add to that finish would only subtract from the overall effect.

End with an image—an image, say, of a cathedral to suggest things lofty—and you give your audience the gift of a takeaway, something they can remember six weeks later. Remember: You are talking to people brought up on TV. When you speak, you, yourself, must in a sense become that TV by telling stories and painting pictures.

At this point, you have armed yourself well to take on even the most challenging speaking assignment. But first, let's take a look at what we've created:

P	*Punch.* Strong start (personal story, illustration, strong statement, rhetorical question, quotation, past, future, humor).
O	*One theme.* One message. (Plus subthemes linked to main theme.)
W	*Windows.* Specific examples to back up your main theme.
E	*Ear.* Speak conversationally. Avoid corporate-speak.
R	*Retention.* End strongly (summary, loop, questions, positive attitude, projection, story).

You may use as many starting methods as you wish to begin, and the same goes for your ending. You may start with a personal story followed by a strong statement, followed by a rhetorical question, for example. And you may end with a repeat of your main point, plus our appeal to the audience, followed by a story.

The POWER Formula is a universal POWER tool for speakers. Plug it into any speaking assignment. Watch your preparation time melt away, leaving you free to do other things. Watch your audience look at you with new interest, wide awake, responding. Watch your POWER go up, while the time it takes to make the presentation goes down. And watch people remember not only the message but also the details of your presentation long after you've given it.

Now it's time to pump *POWER* into your *rocket* and blast off.

C H A P T E R
E L E V E N

GETTING THE
MESSAGE ACROSS

Now that we have *POWER*, the next step is to reintroduce a very old idea: A timeless design that wastes nothing and adds nothing that's not essential. The design I am thinking of here is the *rocket*.

I propose that we picture every talk, lecture, speech, or presentation as a rocket ship—a design elegantly simple, yet manifestly functional. The rocket is designed with minimum air drag, moves very fast, is usually aimed at a target, has a lot of power, and can pack a terrific payload. If more business presentations were designed like rockets, we would waste a lot less time and get a lot more done.

Picture a rocket. In the nose cone you have your all-important message, your theme, which you will launch into the heads of everyone in the audience. Now picture design lines in the fuselage of the rocket which lead from the "warhead" directly down into the body of the ship. At the ends of those design lines are subtopics. Each is connected to the nose cone, and each serves as a kind of separate fuel pod to power the rocket on its way.

Churchill said we can't try to talk about more than one thing at a time. But he also said that if you want to talk about a lot of things, that's all right, too—as long as each subject you undertake to discuss is linked directly to your larger theme. In other words, each subject is just another aspect of your big message. This leaves no room for tangents and discourages redundancies.

So if your theme is the need for globalization, but you also want to talk about research and development, strategic planning, productivity, profitability, sales and marketing, and manufacturing, the design of your rocket may look something like this:

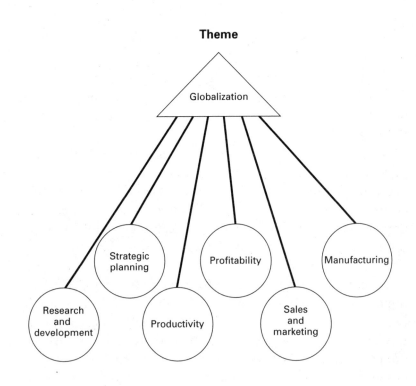

If you were to try to talk about these subjects in a random manner, you would wind up with a random presentation—a presentation of six themes (seven, if you include globalization)—seemingly going nowhere. But by unifying them under a kind of central command, you have turned a jellyfish into a potent missile that you can be sure will have an impact.

By contrast, most business presentations really do seem to go nowhere. Most business presentations I have seen are poorly designed, too long, ineptly delivered, and ultimately forgettable. For all the time committed to preparing them and giving them, too often the presenter would have done better to stay home or send a memo. Rather than enlighten, most presentations irritate, frustrate, and obfuscate. Rather than serving as platforms of opportunity, they can be frequently a kind of professional gallows where we wind up only hanging ourselves. In fact, it is not uncommon for perfectly competent, even talented managers to find that their career paths are suddenly blocked because they seem unable to effectively present themselves or their ideas to others.

One of the beauties of shaping your concepts in the form of a rocket is that the rocket is a unified instrument of pure intellectual energy. All its working parts are strategically connected for maximum impact. Pick any part of our model rocket and you can't have one part without the other. In a sense, the parts act in concert, like a team: one for all and all for one.

Consider, for a moment, the POWER Formula and our presentation which has globalization as its theme. We have talked about how R&D, strategic planning, productivity, profitability, sales and marketing, and manufacturing all relate to globalization. Now let's go one more step and give concrete examples to back up our position (remember that examples are the W in POWER). Add the examples and the design looks like this:

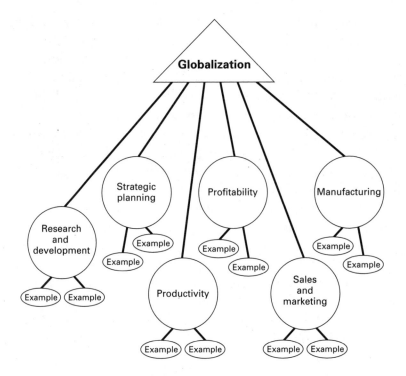

Aside from the remarkable simplicity of the model, three points should come immediately to mind:

1 The rocket has an actual rocket shape. It's streamlined with all the parts fitting together in a very functional way.

2 Everything is headed in the same direction.

3 Everything is connected.

This last point is vitally important. Profitability is discussed only in the context of globalization, and examples are offered only to reinforce profitability. Break that rule at any point in a presentation and the presentation itself will start to lose shape and eventually fall apart.

So you could say that *POWER* is to organization what *rocket* is to streamlined design. *POWER* appeals to the mind. *Rocket* appeals to the mind as well, but also to the curious but enduring notion that all things are really one. When you apply this principle to a presentation, everything—everything—in that presentation is connected.

In other words, rocket and POWER are two aspects of the same thing. At this point we have built a rocket and packed it with POWER.

Now you should be ready to launch at will.

THE NECKLACE

If for any reason the rocket design doesn't do it for you, you might want to consider a more Zen-like bit of imagery: the necklace.

Picture a necklace. The necklace is made of silver thread on which are many pearls. The silver thread is your theme. The pearls are examples which hang on the theme. Just a single message with no subthemes and examples to reinforce that message. The necklace becomes complete when you attach the two ends together and it forms a circle.

I remember a professor in college who once waxed rhapsodic for 55 minutes about the Ralph Waldo Emerson journals and Emerson's almost mystical passion for nature. The rhetoric was eloquent, but the lectures a little thin on example, which made it tough for us students to stay with the professor for more than 18 minutes. I can assure you that today I can remember very little from that course, whereas I am happy to say I can recall much more from courses in which the instructors were wise enough to use illustrations, either verbal or pictorial.

The professor had a silver thread, but no pearls. No necklace.

When I tell people their presentations are too long, the typical reaction is, well, okay, we'll just take out a few examples. Wrong. The better solution is to edit seriously, streamline, avoid redundancies, and *add* examples (which parallels the point we made in the window part of POWER).

This exercise of edit and redesign usually lops off a lot of fat and adds sparkle, with the result that the presentation is shorter and gives more bang for the buck—because the audience now gets the right information in the right way. Ultimately, this transition translates into measurably higher productivity for everybody involved.

Add the rocket and the necklace to POWER and you get:

THE POWER FORMULA

Punch

1. BEGIN WITH THE ENDING (strong statement)
2. PERSONAL STORY
3. ANECDOTE OR ILLUSTRATION
4. RHETORICAL QUESTION
5. QUOTATION
6. PROJECT INTO FUTURE
7. LOOK INTO PAST
8. HUMOR (tell as if true, make business point, don't blow punch line and be appropriate).

One Theme

ONE MESSAGE, ONE MISSION, ONE THEME ONLY. BUT YOU MAY DISCUSS THAT ONE THEME IN MANY DIFFERENT WAYS.

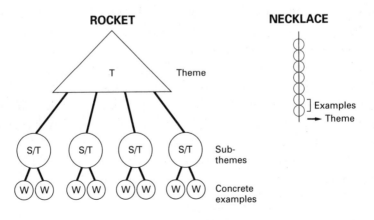

Window

SPECIFIC EXAMPLES, ILLUSTRATIONS AND ANECDOTES TO PROVIDE PROOF.
(This is how you let audiences actually see inside your presentation.)

Ear

STAY CONVERSATIONAL. DON'T SPEECHIFY.

Retention

1. SUMMARIZE KEY POINT OR KEY POINTS—ONE OR THREE. ONE IS BEST.
2. LOOP BACK TO BEGINNING.
3. ASK AUDIENCE TO DO SOMETHING SPECIFIC.
4. APPEAL TO THE POSITIVE.
5. PROJECT AHEAD.
6. TELL A SYMBOLIC STORY THAT EMBRACES YOUR MESSAGE.

CHAPTER

TWELVE

WRITE LIKE YOU SPEAK— 10 IMPORTANT RULES TO LIVE BY

Speaking from a prepared text is sometimes a very good idea and sometimes not such a good idea. But if you must do a prepared text, then it only makes sense that the words in your text are conversational, easy to read, and easy to say.

What you *don't* want is a script that reads and sounds like something out of a trade paper, business review, or somebody's deadly dull memo.

What you *do* want is something that lets you sound like yourself, perhaps even be yourself. And the closest any of us can ever get to sounding like ourselves with a prepared text is to make sure the writing is simple. That's the secret behind every great speech. Every great speech writer knows that the most direct way to the audience's heart and mind is to speak directly. The simply written speech makes it possible for *any* speaker to invest personality into the words, then into the audience.

Most people don't understand the difference between writing for the ear and writing for the eye. Ideally, there is no difference. But for the majority of people there will always be a big difference.

A surprising number of business people write their own speeches. But how they write those speeches makes it virtually impossible for them to look or sound the way they naturally talk. In other words, they defeat themselves even before they begin. Unwittingly, in a sense they create a vehicle without wheels. It's a curious paradox that their own work also becomes the instrument of their potential self-destruction.

The solution is simple: Write the way you speak. To help you write the way you speak, I have assembled a few easy writing rules:

1. *Keep your sentences short.* If you have a sentence with a number of subordinate clauses, break it down into bite-sized pieces. Or break it up with three dots (. . .) placed strategically throughout the long sentence in several places. Or simply translate the long sentence down to a short one. Example:

Too-long sentence: It is necessary to reexamine our intentions vis-à-vis the responsibilities we understand lie ahead, in order that we may have a more disciplined approach to the challenges presented by the new tax legislation, which is presently, in any event, expected to reveal a number of surprises for our members, who can take some comfort in the fact that the tax laws, as we have experienced them in the last five years, have been generally favorable for people in an income bracket exceeding $100,000.

Revised: The tax laws will change, and those changes will have a material effect on each of us.

2. *Choose the active voice.* *Wherever possible, avoid the passive voice.* The passive voice is the voice of the bureaucrat. (Of course, if you want deliberately to obfuscate, then by all means use the passive voice.) The passive voice takes the "actor" out of the action, but the active voice puts the actor back in. Examples:

Passive voice: It is imperative that the defense establishment be refurbished in order that the military operation can be prosecuted.

Revised: Give us the tools and we will finish the job. (Winston Churchill in a letter to President Roosevelt.)

Passive voice: It is obligatory that all illumination be extinguished before the premises are vacated (government bureaucrat).

Revised: Turn off the lights when you leave. (FDR telling government bureaucrat how to translate the above sentence.)

3. Pick short, conversational words. Avoid archaic language that still lingers in the lexicon but is fast on its way out. We are still probably 30 years ahead of ourselves on this one, but I still prefer to err on the side of economy.

Here are some examples:

Old: Notwithstanding our commitment to keep out of the dispute, we should still try to do something to resolve the conflict.

Revised: In spite of our commitment to keep out of the dispute, we should still try to do something to resolve the conflict.

Old: Inasmuch as we are all in this together, we should probably try to cooperate rather than argue.

Revised: Since we are all in this together, we should probably try to cooperate rather than argue.

Old: Therefore we should take it upon ourselves to provide the necessary leadership.

Revised: So we should take it upon ourselves to provide the necessary leadership.

Old: Moreover, we have not yet heard a believable argument from the other side.

Revised: What's more, we have not yet heard a believable argument from the other side.

Old: However, we were unable to reserve a seat for the performance.

Revised: But we were unable to reserve a seat for the performance. (Some people cling to the notion that it is not okay to start a sentence with *but*. This argument was more credible 30 years ago than it is today. I take the position that the language is changing fast and that starting with *but* today is not only permissible, but actually desirable— because it is more conversational, whether in writing or speaking.)

Old: Furthermore, our budget will not allow us to take on an extra project this year.

Revised: Not only that, but our budget will now allow us to take on an extra project this year.

As a rule, speakers should opt for the revised and leave the "dinosaur" words to the lawyers and bureaucrats who are so loathe to give them up. (Which is not to say that if you happen to be a lawyer or bureaucrat you can't also be an effective speaker. But if all lawyers and bureaucrats spoke the way many of them write, we would need professional translators in every courthouse and state capital.)

4. Avoid "buzz words."   Corporate speeches and presentations are often swarming with "bumblebees":

Buzz word: This solution is one which we believe to be *viable.*

Revised: We think this solution will work.

Buzz word: It is necessary that we *interface* with our research and development employees.

Revised: We've got to sit down and talk with our R&D people.

Buzz word: Therefore, we must *maintain a dialogue.*

Revised: So let's keep talking.

Buzz word: The results of our sales survey will *impact* on the bottom line.

Revised: The results of our sales survey will have an impact on the bottom line.

Buzz word: We must garner our *resources* to compete in the marketplace.

Revised: To compete, we've got to spend more money on R&D and on our own people.

Buzz word: With work, we can expect to achieve *superior synergy.*

Revised: We expect a good fit.

Buzz word: One of our goals is to enter into a policy of *empowerment* with our human resources.

Revised: We are going to let our own people make their own decisions and be accountable for the results.

Nobody will exactly fault you for sounding like a bumble-bee—mainly because many others in the organization have probably got the buzz, too. But you can distinguish yourself and become a more believable speaker (while still remaining a team player) simply by shooing the bumblebee out of your language.

5. Be specific. Don't rely on indefinite reference pronouns—the *he's, she's, they's, them's, it's, ones,* and *we's* that clutter our everyday speech. Repetition in prose is a vice that should be avoided. But repetition in *rhetoric* is a *device* that should be encouraged. Examples:

Pronoun: We told *them* that *he* would take *one* to *him,* but *she* said *they* gave *it* to *him,* before *he* had a chance to read *it.*

Specific: Bob and I told the management committee that Dan would take a copy of the document to Tom, but Alice said the board gave the proposal to us before Dan had even read the proposal.

This is an extreme example, perhaps, but it illustrates that important pronouns can easily get lost. It's not uncommon, for example, to be talking about several *him's* at once in the same sentence. Great care should be taken that people always understand exactly whom you are talking about at all times. I have heard reports of more than one deal going sour because the listeners misunderstood the pronoun. Who is "he"? What, exactly, is "it"?

If you are reading a newspaper article, you can follow the reference pronoun, because you need only track back to the top of the sentence to find out to whom the "he" is referring. But when someone is speaking, you have no way of checking the reference—unless you interrupt that person and ask, for example, "What *he* are you talking about?" Common courtesy would restrain most people from asking that kind of question, and you may not know that your listeners are already lost.

I remember once when I sat in on one of my daughter's college classes, the professor's command of his subject profited him little in the face of a daunting barrage of self-inflicted pronouns. He was describing the similarities between Fascism and Communism, with Nazis and Blackshirts in the Fascist camp and Leninists and Marxists in the Communist camp—a total of six separate entities. He paced around the stage talking excitedly about "it," "that," "one," "them," and "they." Individuals melted into "him" and "he." It soon became impossible to figure out who was who and what was what. In the end, after an hour and a quarter, and in spite of his enthusiastic delivery, the students left the room not much more enlightened than when they walked in. That's a waste of talent and time and one case when you can blame a lack of knowledge—not of subject but of the correct use of pronouns.

So repeat the name again and again when you're speaking. Instead of, "We told them that that was one which she said he would give to me," say, "Our firm told the opposing lawyers that this case was the case that Bob's secretary said the boss would give to me." Still convoluted, but a lot clearer than an omelet of indefinite reference pronouns.

6. Avoid sweeping generalities. Sweeping generalities, like sheepdogs, tend to hide more than they reveal. For example:

> *Generality:* Now is the time that this nation should begin thinking seriously again about tapping *alternative energy sources*.
>
> *Revised:* Now is the time to start thinking seriously again about tidal and wind power and solar and nuclear energy.
>
> *Generality:* Now more than ever this country must depend on her *learning institutions* to produce an educated and productive population for the future.
>
> *Revised:* Now more than ever we must depend on our universities, public and private schools, vocational centers, community colleges, hospitals, and corporate training centers to produce an educated and productive population for the future.

The "sheepdog" races in one ear and right out the other. The more "snapshots"—brief concrete images—that you give people, the more likely they are to remember what you said.

7. Don't use confusing words. Some words send out signals that often can be misleading and fuzzy. Examples:

> *Fuzzy:* I would like to *cite* that *site* as just one more example of how we have lost *sight* of our environmental mandate.
>
> *Clear:* That location is just one more example of how we have lost sight of our environmental mandate.
>
> *Fuzzy:* The city building codes require that we *raze* (sounds like raise) all buildings that are beyond repair.

Clear: The city building codes require that we tear down all buildings that are beyond repair.

Fuzzy: I found all the hectic activity leading up to the wedding to be *enervating*. (Sounds like energize, but actually means drain.)

Clear: I found all the hectic activity leading up to the wedding to be exhausting.

Fuzzy: When we hurt the tourist industry, we are in effect cutting off our air line. (Means oxygen hose, but sounds like TWA.)

Clear: When we hurt the tourist industry, we are in effect cutting off our life line.

In the age of AIDS awareness, *conundrum* begins to sound a lot like *condom*. Difficult-to-pronounce words like *conundrum, covetousness,* or *problematic* probably ought to be left out (Jerry Ford couldn't pronounce *nuclear,* so instead had to say *atomic*).

Sometimes words can be used deliberately for whatever reason to send a hidden or tongue-in-cheek message. In his book *The Lexicon of Intentionally Ambiguous Recommendations*, Lehigh University economist Robert Thorton came up with devilishly clever ways to write recommendations for lousy job candidates. For example:

For a candidate with "interpersonal" problems he suggests: "I am pleased to say this person is a former colleague of mine."

For the lazy worker: "In my opinion, you will be very fortunate to get this person to work for you."

For the criminal: "He's a man of many convictions," and "I'm sorry we let him get away."

For the untrustworthy job seeker: "Her true ability is deceiving."

And for the inept worker: "I most enthusiastically recommend this person with no qualifications whatsoever."

Those little beauties are all on purpose, of course, and illustrate the curious ambiguity of the language. But some poor souls put their feet in their mouths and don't even know it. In the *Wall Street Journal,* personnel expert Robert Half noted these clunkers that landed on his desk in star-crossed résumés:

"I am a rabid typist. . . ."

"Thank you for your consideration. Hope to hear from you shorty."

"Here are my qualifications for you to overlook. . . ."

8. Skip the puffed-up, self-serving "peacock" language, couched in superlatives, that strains credulity. I'm talking about the kind of preening talk ("the greatest," "the finest," "the most exemplary") that often finds its way into the canned palaver of elected officials.

Peacock language is: ". . . and I say to you, my fellow Americans, that the time has come for a new day for America, a day of renewed hope and the conviction to meet the challenges of the future." The same old speech. We've all heard it a thousand times.

The same message, couched in more believable language, is: "The worst is now probably behind us. The future won't be easy—no question. But working together, I see no reason why we can't accomplish whatever we make up our minds to accomplish." By toning down the rhetoric we have recast a message of hope into language and terms that people can identify with.

You know you're hearing peacock language when someone says: "It's not the money—it's the principle!" (You know they've already got a hand in your pocket.) Or "To be honest with you . . ." (what have you been the rest of the time, dishonest?). Or when the CEO reminisces about "my best years" spent on the factory floor. Or when the speech writer has the CEO say: "Profits are secondary! What we're really interested in is people. . . ." Or the limousine liberal who flies in from his summer house in the Hamptons to tell an audience: "I can't sleep at nights thinking about the plight of blacks in America."

To be credible, you also must accept the notion that one simple unembellished truth in the right place can carry more weight than a whole marching band of half-truths, euphemisms, unrealistic projections, and promises you know you can never keep. By contrast, just one phony line can drag down the integrity of all the honest lines in the rest of the speech.

We've gotten so used to superlatives, exaggerations, and misrepresentations—especially from political people—that it almost seems natural to stretch the truth. For example, speech writers often stray from the believable by having principals say things like: "This is the greatest experience of my life," when, of course, it is not. *One of the greatest,* maybe. That is unarguable. But *the greatest* strains credibility and tends to taint the rest of what the speaker has to say.

Sometimes exaggerated writing begins to sound like the equivalent of elevator music. We know it's there, but it's so bland we hardly notice it: "The next century will be a time of great economic challenge and opportunity for this nation. If we meet the challenge in a forthright and courageous way we can ascend to even higher levels of prosperity; if we do not, we will slip into a steady decline to economic mediocrity." A better version is: "The next 100 years are critical. In fact, they remind me of the Chinese word for *crisis.* The Chinese use two picture characters to denote the word *crisis.* The picture word for *danger* is placed next to the picture word for *opportunity.* . . . Well, the twenty-first century can be a dangerous time of declining productivity—or a decade of opportunity with new markets and expanded growth."

Résumé writers, too, are legendary in their ability to embellish. The résumé writer will say, "spearheaded marketing, advertising, and new product development." In fact, the writer may have been just one of many marketing people assigned to three or four failed new product launches.

If all speeches told the truth (Churchill: "The news from France is very bad. . . .") we would probably be more productive. And if all résumés were true, we wouldn't have recessions.

9. Avoid weak verbs. *Use stronger, active verbs wherever possible.* Examples:

Weak: Now we must *maintain our resolve.*

Stronger: We've got to keep fighting.

Weak: This year our *growth will be sustained.*

Stronger: This year we'll keep growing.

Weak: We are also going to *reduce costs.*

Stronger: We are also going to cut costs (*cut* for moderate, *slash* for extreme).

Weak: And we expect to *incur a loss.*

Stronger: And we expect to lose some money.

Weak: In the end, we hope to *evince a profit.*

Stronger: In the end we hope to make money.

10. Keep a tight leash on statistics. Statistics tend to proliferate like rabbits in business presentations of all kinds. Polls tell us that audiences can't remember more than one key figure at a time. The ear is not a funnel into which we can pour information like a gas hose overflowing. The ear overloads. It can't digest. Too many facts can defeat the communication.

Some quick tips for rabbit control (managing statistics):

- Pick the most important.
- Round them off.
- Dress them up.

The following are examples of rabbits and their revisions:

Rabbits: Market share increased 3.2 percent, from 5 percent to 8.2 percent in the last quarter, compared to an increase of 4.5 percent, up to a high of 13.5 percent from a low of 9 percent in the same quarter last year. (That's too many numbers for the brain to manage—especially if the rest of the presentation is also liberally laced with statistics. Worse, the construction is clumsy.)

Revised: Market share was off more than 5 percent this year.

Rabbits: Production increased 6.3 percent from 8.1 billion bbl to 10.2 bbl from 1993 to 1994. (Still too much stuff.)

Revised: Production was up more than 6 percent—roughly 2 billion barrels in the last year alone. That's enough oil to heat Boston for 10 years. . . .

We "dress up" the statistic to give meaning to the otherwise meaningless concept of "a barrel of oil." People can't picture 2 billion barrels of oil. So you make an analogy almost anyone can identify with—especially if you are talking to a nonindustry audience.

A good analogy can make all the difference. As a client of mine puts it, a good analogy can "stir the blood." Here's another example:

Rabbits: "Increased productivity worldwide is projected to rise by 2 percent or 99.3 million tons per year in terms of edible grains." This dry little sentence is not only badly written ("in terms of . . ."; passive voice; and "edible grains," a "sheepdog") but also provokes a big "so what?" When we dress it up we might get something like: "Increased productivity world-wide will mean another 2 percent of rice, corn, and wheat a year—roughly 100 million tons. That's enough food to feed every hungry mouth in the Third World for three months."

The food analogy provides not only dramatic perspective and dimension but also the all-important human element that makes the numbers, and the business behind them, seem to come alive.

The insurance industry is notoriously fond of statistics as we can see in the following examples:

Rabbits: During the past five years, property and casualty premiums have grown at a 15.6 percent average compound annual growth rate to $90.1 billion. Personal lines have grown to $38.4 billion (a 14 percent annual growth rate), and commercial lines have grown to $51.7 billion—a 16.7 percent compound annual growth rate.

Revised: During the past five years, property and casualty premiums have grown to more than $90 billion. That's enough insurance to insure every house and car in England. Put another way, if your salary had gone up at the same rate and you were earning $5,000 a year in 1959, today you'd be making $116,000 a year.

Rabbits: The top four firms—of which ours is second—wrote 21 percent of the business. The top eight firms wrote 32 percent, and the top twenty firms wrote 54 percent. The top 50 firms wrote 75 percent of the business.

Revised: We're kind of the "Avis" of insurance. We're only second—but we try harder. The result is that we have a big share of the business. Overall in the industry, the top four firms wrote about a fifth of the business. The top eight firms wrote about a third—and the top twenty firms wrote a little more than half.

THE SIX MOST COMMON LANGUAGE MISTAKES

As far as profits, if we would have kept the factory where it's at, there's three things we should have done in terms of productivity for the managers that have to run it.

Apart from being hopelessly unwieldy, this sentence embraces six of the most woefully abused language mistakes we hear not only in business but in life itself. Four of the six betray the speaker as someone with an incomplete education. The fourth—a numbing reliance on the phrase *in terms of*—just indicates lazy talk (and lazy writing).

Now look at this:

As far as profits *are concerned, if we had* kept the factory where it is, *there are* three things we should have done *to boost* productivity (for the managers who have to run the factory).

You can see that remedying the biggest goofs comes down to a quick fix. (*For the managers who have to run the factory* is unnecessary. I've left it in only to make a point.) Anyone can easily upgrade the quality of their speaking and writing by getting rid of just a few bad habits:

1. *As far as* always requires *is* (or *are*) *concerned* or *goes* to complete the thought or phrase.   It's always got to be as far as something goes or is concerned—not just as far as something. So the sentence above should read, "As far as profits go. . . ." or "As for profits. . . ."

2. *The conditional subjunctive can never be expressed as if I would have* or *if she would have* or *if they would have.*   The correct way to follow *if* is to use *had* with the verb—"If he had"—Or to drop *if* altogether—"Were he to have" or "Had he. . . ." So our sentence should read, ". . . *if we had.* . . ."

3. Just one item or person requires a singular verb; more than one requires the plural. In my opinion, this is the most common rhetorical mistake of our time. For reasons frustratingly unclear, whole generations have fallen to mismatching the verb "to be" with singular and plural nouns. My kids do it, and their kids will probably wind up doing it, too. But it's wrong, and we ought to make every effort to get at least this little thing right.

No more, "there's five people waiting in the conference room." Is it so tough to say, *"there are* five people"? Our sentence should read, *"There are* three things. . . ."

4. *That* is for things. *Who* is for people. Instead of, "This is the woman *that*," simply make it, "This is the woman who." But, "This is the office *that.* . . ." Our sentence should read, ". . . managers *who.* . . ."

5. *In terms of* is just plain tedious. It robs us of whatever action verb or economy of scale we once might have chosen to express ourselves—before we had *in terms of* to fall back on.

Instead of, "We expect to improve, in terms of profits," try, "We expect to make a profit." Instead of, "In terms of labor, we are hiring more people," just say, "We're hiring more people." Instead of, "In terms of outlook, the future is not promising," try, "We could be doing a lot better." In our sentence we seek an active verb. Instead of "in terms of productivity," we choose ". . . boost productivity."

6. Never place an *at* after *where is,* as in, "Where is he *at*?" or, "He knows where it's *at*," or "I know where the files are *at*." How about just: "Where is he?" "He knows where it is." (But if you're trying to be hip, you can leave the *at* in.) "I know where the files are." Our sentence should read, ". . . where it is. . . ."

Actually, our original sentence could come down to this: "If we had stayed, we would have had to boost productivity to increase profits."

If you don't think any of this matters, think again. A junior person from company A makes a sales pitch to a senior person from company B and her staff. Company A doesn't get the order—and will never know why. The reason is that, although the junior person from A was intelligent, apparently competent, and seemingly knowledgeable, he was also to some degree *inarticulate.* The senior person from B comes away with the impression that the person from A is out of his depth, in over his head, a little lacking in sophistication, a little naive perhaps, and (if the way he talked tells us anything) also short on the kind of education that people from B would look for in a business partner or relationship.

Here are a few other bear traps you might want to avoid:

Incorrect: "If I was him. . . ." *Correct:* "If I were he. . . ." (*Were* must follow *if*, and *he* must follow the verb *to be*.)

Incorrect: "You did real good." *Correct:* "You did really well." (*Good* is not an adverb, and you have to throw an *ly* on an adverb that modifies another adverb.)

These are all small fixes that can yield big payoffs. In my experience, the more articulate the presenter, the higher the potential for business success.

It may not be entirely circumstantial that none of the business and political leaders I have known commits *any* of the six most common language mistakes.

PART

THREE

DELIVERY

HOW TO BEAT FEAR

Before you can even think about talking in public, first you must deal with the enemy within: anxiety, self-doubt, stage fright, and all the other little psychic bugaboos that in varying degrees plague most human beings. Not everybody experiences fear of public speaking. But for those who do, performance anxiety can be a major roadblock, and we've got to find a way around it.

> The good news is that fear is not all bad. Fear is the mind's wake-up call: A way to make you more alert, responsive, fine-tuned for action. Fear is part of human nature, altogether natural, and to be expected. But, out of control, fear can overwhelm and paralyze. Utter fear is utterly debilitating, and we must avoid it. The trick is to shape fear and anxiety into a tool put to our good use.

In other words, we don't want to get rid of the butterflies entirely. As a friend of mine puts it, we just want them to fly in formation. And that requires an attitudinal adjustment.

Of course, the best way to conquer fear is to make the same speech 100 times. But let's assume that making the same speech over and over is not a likelihood for most of us. Outside of pharmaceuticals, prayer, or hypnosis, the only way I know to conquer fear is to change the way we perceive public speaking. It's as simple as turning the caveman flight-or-fight mentality of cold sweats and rapid heartbeats into an attitude of positive anticipation and healthy challenge.

In advance of any speaking assignment, you should mentally prepare by reminding yourself of five key points:

1. *Love the people.*   Picture yourself on a familiar footing with the audience. Try to have a prevailing sense of warmth and good will toward the people who have come to hear you speak. Imagine yourself in your own living room or dining room, enthusiastically letting old friends in on an exciting new piece of information. The truth is that most people don't care about how much you know—until they know how much you care. You will be surprised how this single altered perception in itself goes a long way towards defusing your anxieties—and giving you more "energy" than you thought you had.

2. *Serve the people.*   Remember that you have come *in service* to these people in the audience. You have come to serve *them,* not yourself. They have every reason to expect something of value from you (otherwise, why show up in the first place?), and you have a responsibility to give them value. The way to deliver value is to be more concerned about the audience than you are about yourself. Concentrate on the message, not on the messenger. Focus on what you are saying, and you won't have to worry about how you are doing. The measure of how you are doing is proportionate to your commitment to what you are saying.

3. *You're the guru.*   Remind yourself that you know as much or more about your subject than anyone in the room. This should give you the necessary confidence to forge ahead and do well.

4. *Have fun.* Tell yourself that you're having a good time—as laughable as that might sound to the inexperienced. Try out what you learn in this book. See how the things you learn here can make a difference. Look at your speaking assignment as you would any other fun challenge in life—a tennis or golf game, for example. Have a game plan, practice your moves, your timing, your skills. Picture yourself in a one-on-one conversation talking about an exciting subject with an old acquaintance.

5. *Pump yourself up.* Remind yourself of times in the past when you had to speak. You may not have always been perfect. But you survived. Perhaps it went very well, in which case you can congratulate yourself on a job well done and recall what it was like, how it went, what you did right, how you felt afterward.

These mental games may not eliminate all your butterflies, but they should help change anxiety into healthy sense of excitement and challenge, which is the same frame of mind champion athletes cultivate to win in sports.

Now you are ready.

CHAPTER

FIFTEEN

AVOIDING DANGEROUS TRAPS

When you talk about verbal communications, you're also talking about productivity and time management. In the many corporations where I have been a consultant, too often people spend time preparing presentations that are too long, overwrought, poorly designed, poorly structured, and ineptly delivered. The result is not a good use of the audience's time—because typically most people leaving the room can't pass a quiz on what they've just heard.

Worse, I have seen people spend a month preparing for a presentation when two or three days would have been sufficient.

If you tie up 200 or 20 people in a room for several hours to no good end and with nothing to show for it, then you have wasted everybody's precious time—presenter and audience alike. The same can be said for smaller but equally vital business presentations.

A few years ago a vice president of a *Fortune* 10 company spent a solid month preparing for his first big presentation to the chairman. For 30 days he focused his concentration and productivity time into building something he wasn't quite sure how to build.

When the big day finally came, it was the second day of a long, two-day marathon of presentations. The time was 4:50 Friday afternoon. The vice president was so consumed with the moment and the fast-approaching culmination of all his recent efforts that he failed to correctly gauge the mood in the room. He did not notice, for example, that some of the senior officers were stirring restlessly and impatiently glancing at their watches. Even after a forgettable start to his 40-minute plus presentation and the chairman's curt interruption to request that he speed things up and get to the point—because some people had to catch planes—the vice president marched doggedly onward. Apparently fired by fear of failure, and too rigorously prepared to be flexible, he seemed not to have heard the chairman's admonition.

Meanwhile, waves of thinly disguised impatience swept the room. Soon it became apparent even to the hapless vice president that things were threatening to slip out of control. After 10 minutes, when the vice president had apparently still not gotten to the point, the chairman rang down the curtain. He put an end to the meeting, an end to the presentation, and, as it turned out, an end to the vice president's career in the company.

SEVEN KILLER NO-NO'S

The lesson here was a need for flexibility and perhaps even an entirely new approach in a world where change is a daily fact of life and every second counts. Several elements conspired to make things go badly for the V.P.:

First, his presentation was designed improperly. He never would have had the problems he did had he simply reversed the order—in other words, he should have begun with the conclusion. That, after all, is what his audience was waiting to hear—and never did.

Second, he had planned to speak too long—40 minutes. A maximum of 18 minutes, plus 22 minutes of question and answer (Q&A), would have served him better.

Third, he used too many visual aids. Not only that, but he used them incorrectly and picked the wrong ones.

Fourth, he tried to talk about too much.

Fifth, he allowed the presentation itself to dominate every-thing—even himself. He forgot about the big picture, the message, the main points, instead focusing only on the mechanics of trying to tell too much detail—an exercise I liken to trying to force an elephant into a golf bag. The presentation overwhelmed him and subsequently over-whelmed his audience.

Sixth, on top of all that, he had no theme, no "take-away" that you could remember a week later.

Seventh, as if that weren't enough—for all his preparation, his basic lack of faith in his own presentation showed, and he came across as uncomfortable and nervous.

So despite all his best efforts, he failed. Instead of seizing an opportunity, he walked into a series of common traps and wound up a victim of his own undoing. Just a few simple guide-lines, covered in this book, might well have saved the day.

CHAPTER
SIXTEEN

THE 18-MINUTE WALL: AUDIENCE ATTENTION SPAN

All your planning, talents, and good execution will be in vain if you fail to recognize one simple—and critical—law of nature.

In the 1970s the Navy did a study to find out how long people can listen to other people talk. The objective was to best use the time of instructors and students throughout the Navy's education system. The answer surprised a lot of people. The answer was not an hour, or even half an hour. The answer was just 18 minutes. The Navy found that in a classroom, presentation, or lecture environment, an audience's ability to focus on what the speaker is saying, then remember what was said, drops off at 18 minutes like the continental shelf plunging straight down into the abyss. Unhappily, very few people today are aware of that study or the resulting vital number. If they were, we would save tens of millions of wasted hours and untold lost productivity in business in the United States every year.

But what if we are unable, for any number of different reasons, to limit what we must say to 18 minutes? In real life, particularly in business, we find that presentations often go longer than 18 minutes. Frequently we see, for example, board presentations, analyst presentations, and new business presentations running 40 minutes or longer—and it's not uncommon that a presentation can sometimes take an entire morning or afternoon, and even on rare occasions, a full day.

> **Change the medium to break the tedium.**

I see four ways to get around the 18-minute wall:

1 *Go to Q&A (question and answer).* Cover the basics, all the essentials, in 15 minutes, then set aside 30 minutes for Q&A to touch on details and elements that you feel might need further explanation or fleshing out. Q&A, by the way, is your chance to redeem yourself if you feel that the presentation itself did not go particularly well. Most of us tend to be more effective in Q&A, anyway, because Q&A allows us to be most ourselves and most conversational. We can establish a more personal rapport with the audience and reinforce positions that contribute toward whatever objective we may have—whether it is seeking endorsement, demanding a plan of action, enlisting help, or asking permission.

2 *Use another speaker.* Have an associate speak for 2 minutes or so to highlight, clarify, or amplify a particular area of expertise, then the clock starts again with you. You may repeat the process before the next 18 minutes are up, but human nature probably wouldn't allow you to use the strategy successfully a third time.

3 *Show a tape.* Bring along a tape—that shows, for example, your company at a glance, a new manufacturing process, a new research facility going up, a news clip pertinent to the issue at hand, or clips of other speakers—and insert the tape into your presentation at the appropriate time. (This is often not an option for people in financial services.) The tape can run up to 10 minutes or so and be a nice addition to your presentation. Then you can safely continue to talk for another 18 minutes.

4 *Tell a business story a minute.* Borrow a tip from Billy Graham or Bob Hope. I don't mean try to be funny, and I don't mean be overzealous. I do mean do what they do so well—and that is, tell an anecdote every 30 seconds or minute that helps drive home your theme, the point you are trying to make. Whatever anecdote you use—a personal recollection, something you saw on TV or read in the newspapers, something somebody told you—should be aimed squarely at your message, with the specific intention of reinforcing that message. This is why Billy Graham can talk alone on a stage for two hours—because he is talking about a subject which is perceived to be of vital interest to his audience, using well-chosen illustrations to vividly back up the points he is making (all those points, I might add, are not just scattered or used randomly but are linked to one clear theme—in this case, redemption and salvation).

CHAPTER

SEVENTEEN

HOW TO CAPTURE YOUR AUDIENCE

TWO BIG 8'S

THE 8-SECOND FAST START

Keeping the important 18-minute wall in mind, we now have to consider the fast start 8-second rule. The 8-second rule appeals to a simple law of human nature which suggests that most people decide within 8 seconds whether a particular speaker is worth listening to in the first place. In other words, don't piddle away your moment of greatest impact on opening amenities. Opening amenities are opening inanities.

So begin *strongly*. Avoid anemic cliché starts such as: "Thank you. Good morning. It is a pleasure to be here today. . . . Today I would like to talk about. . . ." Most presentations, talks, lectures, and speeches—an overwhelming majority—do begin that way. But that is not necessarily a good reason to do so ourselves. In fact, it is probably a compelling reason *not to*, since one way we can distinguish ourselves is through our uniqueness.

No one will fault you for saying, "Thank you." That's fine. "Thank you" is cordial. But skipping the thank you and getting right at it is, in my view, even better.

Good managers value differences even in a team environment. Who will criticize us for being different if being different means we can also be more effective?

THE 8-SECOND DRILL

Of all the virtues that a good speaker brings to the party, none is more highly prized than brevity. A century ago, Mark Twain got a telegram from a publisher. The telegram read: "Need 2-page short story, two days." Twain wired back: "No can do 2 pages two days. Can do 30 pages two days. Need 30 days do 2 pages."

Shorter is sometimes harder. But shorter is also usually better, because it concentrates essential information into a narrower space, thereby casting a brighter light on the subject and cutting down the time we need to listen.

The ability to focus information into ever-smaller time slots is a skill essential to our time. For example, a friend of mine was summoned to his boss's office for a meeting that was supposed to take about a half an hour. But as my friend got off the elevator he found his boss heading for another elevator and beckoning my friend to join him.

Something urgent had come up, the boss explained. My friend now found himself having to distill a half hour into the 20 seconds it took the elevator to reach the ground floor. He had to figure out his bottom line, edit and review it in his mind to make sure he left nothing out and added nothing extraneous, then sum it all up crisply, clearly, and with confidence.

Happily, this was no problem, because he had already worked with me to sharpen his powers of concentration on what I call the *8-second drill*.

The *8-second drill* is an exercise my clients experience in the course of their speaker training. But anyone can practice the *8-second drill* at home. Here's how it works:

1 Pick a timely or pressing business topic to talk about for 3 minutes. Take a position. Have an opinion. Don't just narrate a list of facts or a historical chronology or a loose set of concepts without evidence to back them up. For example, instead of talking about "Globalization in the next century" talk about "Our survival as a nation may depend on our ability to dominate global markets in the next century." That's a position. That's leadership.

2 Present your case. Write down some ideas. Set up a logical course to follow. Detail the steps you plan to take, then set your notes aside. With your ideas all in a row and fresh in your head, stand in front of a mirror or a portable TV camera and start talking. Allow yourself not even 1 second more than 3 minutes.

3 Now take 1 minute off your time and do the same thing in 2 minutes. Then go to 1 minute, 30 seconds, 20 seconds, 10 seconds, and finally 8 seconds.

The hardest part is from 30 seconds on down. When you get to 20 seconds you are in the neighborhood of the typical 18-second "sound bite" broadcasters talk about. Ten seconds is a real crunch, and 8 seconds is about as far as any human being can reasonably be expected to go.

When you finally break through to 8 seconds, you will have captured the absolute essence of what you are talking about. This single statement, phrase, or idea embraces your theme. It is your message. Frequently, when people tell me they don't know what their theme is, I tell them to try the 8-second drill. Your message, whatever it may be, cannot hide in the spotlight of the 8-second drill.

You can be certain that the ultimate truth will come out every time—provided it is subjected to the rigors of the 8-second drill. The 8-second drill answers the question, what am I really talking about here? It will demand—and get—the distilled product every time.

REVERSING THE WAVE

The 8-second drill is a function of "reversing the wave"—that is, getting to the point right away. Some lawyers, accountants, sales people, and others are accustomed to taking their time to explain themselves by typically building to an elegant conclusion or building their point in the shape of a wave. If they are oblivious to the 18-minute wall and don't know how to get over it, anyway, they might drift unaware into dangerous territory and never know why they did not get the order.

When you "reverse the wave" you slash that risk by getting to the point almost immediately. So if you are cut off or interrupted, or you unexpectedly run out of time, you can take some comfort in the knowledge that your message is already on the table. And if you are not cut off, you can relax a little and spend the rest of the time surfing down the back side of the wave and explaining how you came to your conclusion.

The 8-second drill makes it possible to know exactly how you should begin. In fact, it provides three functions:

1 The bottom line (your message)
2 The top line (your mind grabber)
3 The last line (your takeaway)

Once you know the real point you're trying to make, then you can also begin and end with that point (leaders often recognize the psychological advantages of this most basic and simple form of reinforcement and explain what they want—a plan of action, for example—at the beginning as well as at the end). Start and finish are the theme.

If we look at the globalization example mentioned a moment ago, and apply the 8-second drill, the "top line" equals the "bottom line" equals the "last line." All the lines are one: "Our survival as a nation may depend on our ability to dominate global markets in the next century." That's the point, the essence, the thing itself—the hard nut that tells it all. Big concept, few words, bullseye. From this single line you can build a rocket ship or a necklace.

The 8-second drill on a speech about nuclear weapons in the post–Cold War period might be: "The most dangerous single threat to civilization is the spread of atomic bomb technology to the Third World."

The 8-second drill about a local pollution problem might be: "Our river is dying. We have got to take action now to save it—before it's too late."

Interestingly, when people have experienced the 8-second drill in a training session—driving from 3 minutes down to 8 seconds—they become amazed at how many unnecessary words they commonly use to talk about even the simplest subjects. They are even more surprised when they try to reverse the process—pushing back out to 3 minutes from 8 seconds—often finding it is actually difficult to go beyond 40 seconds.

The 8-second drill tells us that we could all be a lot crisper. Crispness makes important information easier and quicker to give, easier to get, and a lot easier to retain. Crispness saves time, enhances productivity, and helps leaders lead.

CHAPTER
EIGHTEEN

KEEP THE MOMENTUM GOING

Adolf Hitler's first speech to the German Bundestag in 1933 is a wonder to behold. The new chancellor stands in silence for several minutes in front of an expectant crowd. He has no lectern, just a few notes on a low table at his side. Long after you would have expected him to say something, he is still standing there, his hands folded in front of him, surveying the crowd in the wordless, speechless, silent chamber.

Minute after minute passes, and still he says nothing. The sense of anticipation builds. There's a muffled cough. More silence. Why isn't he speaking? Now the nervous energy in the room is so supercharged, the air itself seems ready to explode.

Only then does Hitler finally open his mouth and begin to speak—slowly, deliberately, looking hard at the audience, pausing for emphasis. Listeners are devouring every word.

He begins softly but forcefully, obviously not in a hurry, and after a couple of minutes he's starting to hit his stride, building up steam. As the momentum mounts like an ocean swell, the audience is rapt—a sea of fawning faces utterly seduced. Wide-eyed and now almost hypnotized, they begin to ride the wave, carried along by the sheer force of POWER building on the stage.

From that point on, the speaker's pace and energy continue to grow. Fifteen minutes later, the grim little man with the mustache is consumed entirely by his message, forging ahead in a kind of altered state that blends passion and conviction to new heights this audience has never experienced before. They are drawn down into his black hole like feckless flecks of iron dust to a giant magnet. By the time he is finished, he is trembling in a climax of contained frenzy, and they are on their feet erupting in an orgy of applause and adoration. Anyone stumbling into the room at that very moment would swear that something very primal, very earthy, very sexual, like a mass orgasm, had occurred.

And so it had.

Just 15 minutes after whipping the Bundestag into a psychological frappé, Hitler was huddling privately with his closest cronies, calmly analyzing which phrases worked, which didn't, which part of the speech could have been cut or strengthened, where he should have paused longer, and more.

Among other things, Hitler understood that to keep the party going, you've got to build excitement. He knew that an essentially "flat" speech—with the same energy level in the beginning, middle, and end—runs the risk of sagging, usually toward the finale.

> The danger zone typically occurs as we approach the 18-minute wall (Chapter 16), often because most people fail to sustain their energy and momentum. They begin to falter two-thirds to three-quarters of the way through their speech.

Even within the limits of the 18-minute wall, the danger zone is a very real threat. It can unravel any presentation but is most damaging in the prepared text speech. And it can happen for any number of different reasons, sometimes in combination:

1 The presentation itself is badly designed—with a lot of flab evident in the standard sink hole that usually shows up somewhere in the last one-third.

2 The presenter gets bored (particularly if the material itself is boring or the presenter is giving someone else's presentation)—and the lack of interest shows.

3 Most people who are not professional or experienced speakers will by nature begin to flag after the halfway mark.

4 Nervousness cripples the entire presentation.

No one is suggesting that Hitler is a good role model. His blatant theatrics would for the most part bomb in business, especially in the United States. But he understood human nature well enough to almost destroy the civilized world—and therein lies a lesson. The lesson is simple: If you have something worth saying, let your conviction and enthusiasm show. If you let your convictions and enthusiasm show, the danger zone will go away, and the problem will fix itself. The danger zone goes away when your message carries the day—that is: know what you are talking about, translate what you know into a message people can understand, then let that message build in power and intensity throughout your presentation.

Don't worry whether you are too impassioned or too little impassioned. That's not important—leave acting to actors. What's important is first having a message, then believing in it, then giving that message to the audience in a way that leaves no doubt about your total involvement, commitment, and absolute sincerity. Do that and the danger zone will quickly become a safety zone.

But not everybody finds that easy to do. CFOs and their staffs, for example, often object when I encourage them to seek a theme or a message, even in quarterly review. The *review* is the message, they tell me.

Yes and no, I say. Yes, because a review is a review. But no, because a review of any kind is also an opportunity to position the report in a larger, more relevant framework that requires the perspective of leadership. For example, what are the market trends driving the quarter? What changes have emerged that might alter the business? What worldwide long-term trends are in play that will affect the numbers, and why? And, above all, where are we going? What is going to happen? What should we do?

So I tell them: Start by projecting the future, which is what their listeners are *really* interested in. Articulate the business as you see it in the months ahead, *then* explain that projection based on your conclusions and proposals drawing from the previous quarter. This is what we defined in an earlier chapter as "reversing the wave." In effect, start with the ending, then, as if on a backward wave, *build down* (surf down?) toward your ending. That's the opposite of how most presentations are set up. If you were to put it on a graph, it might look like this:

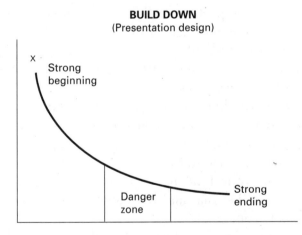

BUILD DOWN
(Presentation design)

Now consider what we've been talking about in this chapter—the danger zone. To get rid of the danger zone, we've got to *build up*. We've got to get the ball going, then kick it *uphill*. In other words, energy goes *up*.

The next figure shows where you can expect to find the danger zone and how your energy and enthusiasm should carry you *upward* through your presentation.

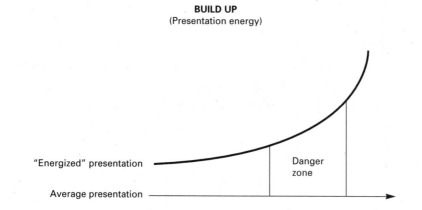

BUILD UP
(Presentation energy)

"Energized" presentation

Danger zone

Average presentation

Now it's plain to see that although presentation *design* operates on the principle of a *reverse* wave, the *energy principle* operates on the principle of a *standard* wave. This may seem like a paradox, but together they combine to create a powerful piece of work, which looks like this:

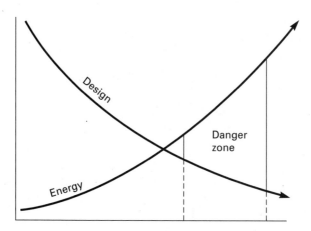

Design

Danger zone

Energy

Now you can forget all this and remember only that the good presentation has a good, strong start in its design and a good, strong ending in its energy. To blow away the danger zone, simply:

1 Be prepared.

2 Apply the POWER formula.

3 Care a lot about what you are saying and not so much about how you are doing—and make sure you do not flag in the final portion of your presentation.

C H A P T E R

N I N E T E E N

THE POWER OF SILENCE

Silence is an asset, rather than a liability—as the rogue German chancellor effectively demonstrated in the last chapter.

Most beginning speakers view complete silence of any kind in a presentation as an anathema. But every good speaker knows how to use silence to his or her advantage. A wise person once said that there is, in any good speech, a greater message in the pauses than in the words that surround them. There may be some truth to that. For one thing, most speakers tend to talk too fast. One reason they speak too fast is because they are always rushing to fill the dreaded "dead air," these moments of sweat-inducing silence when not a sound is occurring in a room filled with people. Another reason is that they want it over with as quickly as possible.

A friend of mine has a recurring nightmare in which he is standing in front of an audience of blank faces, unable to make words come out of his mouth. Nothing, not a sound. Only silence. He wakes up in terror, his heart pounding, and finds it hard to go back to sleep.

This is a person like so many others, who is terrified of public speaking. A famous poll, which I touched on earlier, found that the number one fear of most people is not death, but public speaking. Death was second or third on the list. So we still have a pretty big problem here. A problem big enough in some cases to effect our productivity, our sense of self-worth, and sometimes even our jobs.

But silence and pauses—the biggest perceived demons in public speaking—need never be our enemies. In fact, they can be our very good friends. Actors understand the value of silence better than the rest of us; they know that pauses can make the difference between a mediocre performance and a great one. What separates the men from the boys, so to speak, in public speaking, is what I call the *perception-of-time gap*. More on that shortly.

The strongest start of all is silence.

First, going back to strong starts, the best way to begin strongly is to begin with nothing. That is, look around the room at your audience, look into their eyes, let the seconds tick by until they are convinced you are going to tip over and have a stroke. Stand in utter silence for 4, 5, or 6 seconds, and your silence will fill the room and focus the attention of all the people on you. Where others might begin to prattle nervously, you just stand and say nothing. The sense of anticipation builds through a seeming eternity of passing seconds until at last you say something. And what you say, as you saw in the POWER formula, will further grab their attention. You will begin strongly. You will deliver something of value to them right off the bat.

So silence should occur even before you speak. All the above should happen within our guideline 8 seconds.

THE PERCEPTION-OF-TIME GAP

When I videotape clients speaking, often they cannot believe that the pauses which felt like ages actually look comfortable, conversational, and normal on the tape replay. There is, then, a

---

large gap between the perception and the reality, which we will call *perception-of-time gap,* a faceless, elusive enemy which we have to tame into submission—or it will rise up to threaten us every time we speak.

I remember being in a motorcycle accident some years ago. The time I was actually in the air seemed like 8 or 10 seconds, yet the real time could not have been more than a second.

In a sense, public speaking for some people is kind of like a controlled motorcycle accident. The higher the anxiety, the more time seems to stretch.

In moments of crisis time can appear almost to stand still. Actually, the mind is trying to give the body time to save its own life. Some people call this altered state a heightened sense of "flight or fight." In extreme cases, there may even be enough time to see your life pass before your eyes.

Understanding that the perception-of-time gap lurks within is essential in mastering the art of public speaking and coming across as a leader.

Don't let discomfort with silence dictate your performance. Fight back the need to race on. Cool it. Slow down. Learn to love those weird and wonderful pauses. If you say something important, for example, just stop. Count to three. Look at the people. You'll be surprised how well pauses actually work:

We have got to take action now. Pause.

Each of us is essential to the success of this company. Pause.

We will never surrender! Pause.

Control time and you will control your audience.

CHAPTER
TWENTY

YOUR IMAGE: BODY LANGUAGE AND HOW TO DRESS

I recently watched a senior businessperson extol the virtues of his company to a large audience. Every time he said "me" or "us" he seemed to slap his chest. Twice he struck the lectern with his fist to make a point, but his timing was off, and his points fell embarrassingly flat. Once or twice he said "you"—speaking to the audience—and suddenly thrust his hands out like an evangelist saving souls.

On top of that, he read his speech with his eyes down most of the time.

It was clear to me that someone had tried to train this man to speak and botched the job. The exec wound up looking self-conscious, rigid, and robotic with the result that in spite of all the apparent training he did not go over well with his audience.

When you don't go over, neither does your message.

The key to looking and sounding natural—in other words, conversational—is to try to *be* natural. People have to move in a way that is true to themselves. That's why it can sometimes be more harmful than helpful to try to tell someone to behave or act or move in a given way for a particular situation. When trainers like myself try to coach people to react to the words and ideas they are saying, too often the result makes the client look trained—as was the case with our hapless executive.

> To understand body language, it is first essential to be aware that no set of guidelines is necessarily true for you and that the only real answer to how you should act is within yourself. (When leaders speak, they look animated and relaxed. They seem to respond naturally to whatever they are saying. So can you.)

So the first rule of body language is that there are no rules (short of not acting silly or unnatural, or creating glaring distractions).

The second rule of body language is: Try to answer your own heart when you speak. If you are speaking from a prepared text, for example, try to say the words on the page as if they really were your own and were coming right out of your head (more on prepared text in the next chapter). That's exactly what every good prepared text deliverer needs—a confident conversational style with a thinking person's text and reactions that come from the heart. Even if you can summon no emotion at all, still try to "hear" the words in your head before you actually say them. That way, you are far less likely to sound like you are reading.

If you are speaking extemporaneously or from simple notes, it is a lot easier to practice a "natural" approach, because you don't have to read the speech. Now you can express every idea any number of different ways, with one way not necessarily any better than another. You can be free to warm to your subject and really be yourself.

The natural approach is always the best. Here are a few universal truths that will make any speech delivery better from a podium.

1 Don't sway—keep your feet fairly close together. Swaying only makes you look distracted and uncomfortable—and in a hurry to finish.

2 Turn your feet slightly to face different parts of your audience—sort of pivoting or rotating on the same spot.

3 Keep your head in the same place—which will happen automatically if you don't sway and if you rotate slowly on the same spot under your feet. (If you choose to leave your script behind and walk around, walk slowly, stand up straight—and of course don't worry about keeping your head in the same place.)

4 Use your hands to help animate your talk. I tell my clients to use short chops of their hands for emphasis and to use grander, larger gestures (if they feel comfortable with that) to make important points. You can also hold a pen in your hand to give your hands something to do other than folding them across your groin or falling completely limp to your sides. Touch your hands together, open them up, keep them moving. You might let one hand slip into your pocket while using the other to help you make a point, then switch the free hand into the other pocket and bring the other hand out. If all of the above seems awkward or uncomfortable, then seek your own counsel and trust your own instincts to tell you what to do, and when.

The best way to learn the game is to practice. Use the camcorder, use the mirror. Try to develop a conversational style that feels comfortable. Then apply what you've learned in this book and see for yourself how a little practice can go a long way.

HOW TO DRESS

Like it or not, first impressions often count for a lot—so people could get the wrong idea of what you're all about just by looking at you. That's why it only makes sense to dress in a way that creates a minimum of distraction from your message and at the same time enhances how you want the audience to consider you.

The quick answer to dressing up for the occasion is to wear better-quality clothes that are both simple and basically conservative.

Clearly, this would be the wrong advice for a clown or comedy act or for an informal party atmosphere. But if you're talking about speaking to civic, government, church, or business groups, you can't go wrong by toning down your apparel.

This means that men, in general, would be safe wearing:

1 *Better-quality business suits* (dark blues or shades of grey).

2 *White dress shirts* preferably without button-down collar (plain collar is more elegant). White is a universal fashion standard and offends almost no one. It's even okay to wear on TV—though for years white shirts tended to "flare" and "ghost" on TV screens. Today the technology is so advanced that white is all right. White also defines good skin color contrast—especially in those wan winter months when many of us who happen to be Caucasian tend to lose that healthy outdoor glow. An alternative is pale blue, with or without pinstriping.

3 *Dark knee-length sheer socks* in blue or black (you don't want those pasty, hairy calves poking out at the audience

while you're waiting on a panel for your turn to speak. Nor do you want those calves showing when you cross your legs in a TV interview).

4 *Black shoes only, please,* for blue, pinstripe, or dark grey suits. Brown shoes go better with brown suits, lighter greys and pastels. And while you're at it, make sure your shoes are well-shined and appropriate. In most occasions, lace business shoes are better than loafers, for example. Scuffed, obviously cheap shoes may give some people an excuse to form an early, and perhaps unfair, opinion that you might not be able to shake—no matter what you say or how well you think you speak.

5 *Conservative tie*—small polka dots, solid color, or regiment stripe. Styles come and go, but these old stand-bys seem to go on forever. They look smart and keep distractions to a minimum. For years, consultants like myself have been advising client to wear bright red ties, a bolt of color, which draws the audience's attention right to the face and spotlights the speaker. You can see our political clients almost every day on TV following our advice. But you can also see these people, sometimes three in a row, wearing white shirts, red ties and dark suits all at a table facing the camera in a *Today Show* interview, for example—and you almost expect one to cover his eyes, another his ears, and the other his mouth. So the "power dressing" combo of yesteryear (red tie, white shirt, dark suit) may not be the ticket for the twenty-first century.

Keep in mind that the suit jacket comes off and the sleeves get rolled up when you want to give a nonverbal message of informality—down on the factory floor, for example.

The bottom line is that common sense will dictate what is appropriate. Polyester and pastels are probably best left out of any haberdashery equation (if you look like a lawyer or banker you might be forgiven, but a leisure suit can be seen as a crime against all reasonable definitions of good taste).

We should note here that good-sized portions of the U.S. Midwest view pinstripe suits and the like with special disdain, so a relaxation of the above-suggested guidelines might be in order depending on the particular location in which you find yourself speaking. It might even be a good idea to ask the opinion of someone who is going to be in your audience and be guided by his or her suggestions. (I remember being told by more than one person in the Midwest that I looked exactly like what I was—a fairly facile, somewhat sophisticated Eastern Ivy League City Slicker. I needn't add that this sort of thing does not sit well with a great many people west of the Hudson River. The fact that I did not necessarily sound like a City Slicker—particularly a New York City Slicker—held little sway with these good people, and I'm sure they put me down as someone capable of a good bit of white-collar crime.)

Where the weather is warmer in the South and the Southwest, fabrics get lighter. The darker colors of the Northeast power corridor (Washington-New York-Boston) tend to fade the farther west and south you go, until the transformation is complete in places like Texas, New Mexico, and Arizona, where the suits seem to blend right into the desert landscape.

Another area in which the rules, such as they are, may change is academia—which is notorious for rumpled geniuses and beret-capped professors in ancient tweeds, long scarves, and baggy corduroy pants. Still, when I speak to business school audiences, I stick to my standard bankers-issue dress code, and that seems to be all right. The students or executive program people expect someone who looks like a business consultant, and that's pretty much what they get—but you won't find a lot of professors who dress for the job the way I do.

We should also mention that in recent years Hollywood has brought us pony tails and baggy Italian drape suits, sneakers, shades, jeans, T-shirts and tuxedo jackets for formal evening wear, and a lot of artsy black ensembles for day or night. Comfortable stuff, no doubt, and some of it not bad looking, either. But you've got to be an acknowledged eccentric, or the best in the world at what you do, or independently wealthy to be able to imitate Jack Nicholson or Don Johnson in front of a business audience. Leave the black silk shirt and high tops in the closet.

However, hundreds of companies have taken to designating Fridays as a day of casual dress code, so the times they are a-changing (but if you are scheduled for a business meeting with a client on a "casual" day, you should still wear a suit and tie unless specifically requested not to).

There are whole sections of California, most notably Silicon Valley, where any pretense at conventional business dress went out the window years ago. If you go to Silicon Valley on business, it's best to call ahead and ask what your client thinks is appropriate—particularly if you plan to make a speech or give a presentation. However, San Franciscans—especially those in financial services—tend to dress like New Yorkers.

Women who speak a lot either in business or in politics seem to prefer conservative business suits. Barring that, they will generally opt for dresses that look expensive yet give no suggestion that the wearer is trying in any way to appear sexy. Of course, naturally presentable women cannot help that they do, in fact, sometimes look attractive to men in their audiences—but no woman speaker in her right mind, even in our politically correct times, should lose any sleep over that simple truth or consciously try to change it. Common sense demands, for example, that the neckline not distract.

Women speakers' business suits tend to span a wider color spectrum than those of their male counterparts. Pastel colors, for example, are not uncommon. Bold reds and blues are the most popular of the bright colors.

Hemlines go up and down, but the best-dressed and most experienced women speakers seem to be telling us:

1 Keep it simple—stick to conservative suits and dresses in solid colors.

2 Reduce jewelry to a minimum, thereby cutting down on distractions from the face and eyes.

3 Go easy on eye makeup.

4 Don't wear hats when you speak—unless you are outside.

5 Use scarves whenever appropriate to add a certain flair and style of your own without appearing to be too fashion-conscious.

Over the years, many of my corporate clients have been women who have on occasion expressed personal concerns about speaking in public. Some have confided to me, for example, their discomfort about having to follow a particularly robust, commanding male speaker. They know, correctly, that their voices are not as deep or resonant and perhaps do not carry as well. The contrast, they are afraid, will not only diminish what they have to say but also heighten the potential that the audience may take away an incorrect perception that the woman speaker lacks leadership, strength, or other qualities. These concerns are all understandable and legitimate. But they are also manageable.

First, it is true that any speaker, male or female, who seizes and practices the simple protocols in this book, can fare better than all but the most dynamic speakers—sometimes even without formal training. That's the first point.

The second point is that the soft voice, if used correctly, can be as imposing as the deepest of baritones. That's why God created microphones. I encourage my female clients to make certain in advance that the microphones work well wherever they have to speak. Some of the better mikes do not have to be any closer than 2 feet to pick up and amplify even the gentlest voice. If my female clients have to speak without a mike, I ask them to get as physically close as possible to their audience and then bring their voices up "short of a shout"—that is, speak loudly enough so that they can still look and sound natural and at the same time be heard by even the people in the back row. A number of experienced women politicians know how to do this very well. Naturally, if you go beyond "short of a shout," you will, in fact, be shouting, and that is not desirable.

Volume and projection, then, are fixable. But a slightly tougher problem is presented by the client whose voice falls into a soprano register—what one woman client ruefully calls her "Mickey Mouse" voice. The truth is she does not sound like a Disney character, but her voice is by nature more highly pitched than the average female voice and stands out sharply in every business meeting and every presentation.

In the end, I referred her to a voice coach, who changed my client's breathing and rate of word delivery and helped her come down a notch or two on the falsetto register. This added depth and also beefed up her volume, so that today she feels a lot more self-assurance when she's called on to speak.

Asking clients to boost their volume "short of a shout" is about as far as I am willing to go on the subject of projection. Someone without any real speaking experience, stage experience, or theater training can only sound inadequate or unnatural when trying to project their voice with too much gusto. So if you find yourself in a big room with a lot of people and no microphone, don't overdue it. Remember:

Say it with clout just short of a shout.

TWENTY-ONE

HOW TO READ A PREPARED TEXT LIKE A PRO (AND NOT LOOK LIKE YOU'RE READING)

Prepared text does not make sense for everyone. For most people, speaking from notes or outline or even extemporaneously is more effective and certainly more believable. But sometimes prepared text is the clear choice. For example, when:

- The legal beagles insist you say every word on the page.

- There is a consistent party line that everyone in your organization has to adhere to.

- You have a precise time slot to fill.

- You have no preparation time, and the speech is prepared for you by someone else, or you find yourself having to give someone else's speech.

- Your speech has an accompanying slide show requiring rehearsal and precise cues.

- You feel more confident and comfortable reading from a text than trying to speak extemporaneously or from notes or outline.

Reading from a script while trying to appear *not* to be reading is a neat trick. But that is exactly what we have to do if we expect people to take us seriously and be willing to listen to what we have to say.

Few people—either in public or private life—know how to handle a prepared text properly. Unless they are using TelePrompters, even U.S. presidents look like they are reading a text verbatim.

No one can master the art of prepared text delivery from a book—because until now no book has been able to explain correctly how it should be done. But a few simple tips, plus some practice in front of a mirror, can still make a measurable difference in how you come across.

DON'T SHOOT 'TIL YOU SEE THE WHITES OF THEIR EYES

The key to great prepared text delivery is disarmingly simple. Most people, when they speak from a script, begin almost every sentence with their face and eyes pointed down at the page. They come up for air in the middle of the sentence, then dive right back down to catch the words at the end of the sentence. Repeat this action three or four hundred times and you've got a pretty dull presentation. Graphically, this looks like:

Eyes Up "FOR AIR"

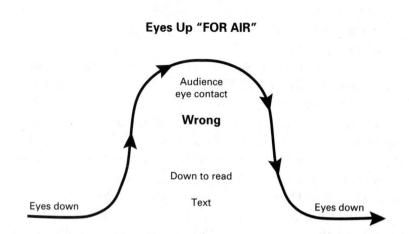

Even if the words are great, the speech will fail in the presentation.

The answer is to reverse the procedure. *Instead of starting each sentence with your eyes on the text, begin each sentence actually looking straight at the audience. Then allow your eye to scan down to read the middle of the sentence right off the page. Then bring your eyes back up to end each sentence looking back at the audience again.* Repeat that several hundred times and you will not look like you are reading the speech. The correct way looks like this:

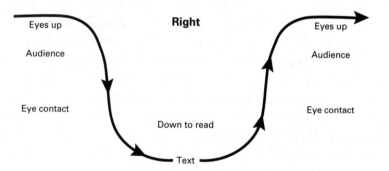

If you like, choose a few faces in the audience all the way from your left to your right and spend a few seconds with each face, one at a time, every time you make eye contact.

So instead of *down-up-down* you are now doing *up-down-up*.

The trick is to allow your eye to memorize the first half or so of the sentence in silence. Then you *bring your eyes up, establish eye contact, and speak the words. Before you run out of words, you allow your eye to return again to the sentence, picking up where you left off and reading the middle of the sentence right off the page. Then you raise your eyes again to finish the last part of the sentence.* All this you do in one seamless sweep with no pauses. The only times you pause are after you establish eye contact (for just a beat, to make sure you don't "cheat" by speaking before your eyes are all the way up) and after each sentence (for emphasis and to make sure you don't dive down for the next sentence before you're finished speaking).

The chances are that you will be speaking too fast, because your mouth will be tempted to try to catch up with your eyes, so *always leash yourself in.*

Consciously slow down, and you will probably wind up sounding conversational.

And remember to *pause often. Pause* after every sentence. *Stop* after every key point. Saturate your audience with eye contact. Really look at the people, and not over their heads.

If you do look over their heads, you may appear to be detached—as if you were trying to remember something (but if you can't bear to face an audience eyeball-to-eyeball, it is always better to look over their heads rather than down at the lectern). Look over their heads and you are in the *ozone.* Look down at your text, the lectern, or your feet, and you are in the *no zone.*

Look them right in the eye, and you are in the *go zone.* The longer you stay in the *go zone*, the better your presentation will be.

TEXT

The up-down-up drill sounds easy, but for people not used to it, it can feel awkward. To make the procedure as easy as possible, prepare your scripted speeches so that:

1 *The letters are big enough to be read easily from 3 to 4 feet away.* Laser printers can quickly produce enlarged conventional typeface which should be ⅓- to ½-inch high.

2 *Each sentence is a separate paragraph.* (This makes it a lot easier to execute the drill we just discussed.) If the original text has several sentences in a paragraph, you can indicate which separated sentences belong to the original paragraph by not indenting those sentences. They would still be separate, just not indented on the speech copy. The only indented sentence would be the lead sentence of the original paragraph.

3 *Double-space each sentence and triple-space each paragraph.*

4 *The last sentence on the page should end on the page.* The sentence should never continue on to the top of the next page (again, easier to track with your eye).

5 *Put page numbers in* ALL FOUR CORNERS. (Life being what it is, you want to avoid having to genuflect for 5 minutes if you should drop your speech on the way up to the podium).

You will now have more pages, but you can easily move each page with almost no distraction by sliding the page while looking at the audience as you speak the words from the last sentence on that page.

When you are ready to go, your pages should look something like this:

We are who we are, and that's
as it should be.

But most of us live our whole lives
not having a clue about who we might
have been.

One way to find out who we might
be is to venture outside our own
expectations . . . to make new
footsteps.

That's what good speakers do . . .
they surprise themselves, and then
they begin to find themselves.

PREPARED TEXT BASICS

- Use large laser print easy to read from at least 3 to 4 feet away.
- Use *upper* and *lower* case.
- *Separate* each *line* with double-space, each paragraph with triple-space.
- Make *every sentence* a separate paragraph.
- Put page numbers in all four corners.

POSITION

Position yourself slightly *away* from the lectern. You don't have to go to MIT to figure out that the angle of attack for your eye is less steep the further back you go. This lets you keep your chin and face up while your eyes go down to the page and do all the work. Your eyes, remember, track down to the page *only* in the *middle* of sentences. Short sentences are simple, you just take them in their entirety.

Just by standing back a few inches you automatically increase your eye contact. You should be away from the lectern 12 to 18 inches, far enough to let you express yourself with your hands if you wish to, yet close enough to still touch the lectern (many people like the comfort of feeling "grounded" to something solid).

Some lecterns are adjustable. If you know in advance you are going to use a prepared text, you should make it a point to request an adjustable lectern. This is particularly important for tall people. Adjust the lectern so that the top of the front is just below your sternum (and just below where your heart is).

HANDS

Short of creating a distraction, try to let your hands help you express yourself, for two reasons:

1. Freeing up your hands to "talk" with you helps vent the anxieties that you may feel about speaking in the first place. People experience anxiety or stage fright in different ways. But allowed to build without release, anxiety can reveal our fear by making us look nervous or wooden. Nervousness often manifests itself as rocking or swaying. Using your hands helps hide fear by physically releasing tension.

Of course, your hands should not run away with you. They should always help, never distract. So keep your moves disciplined: short chops to make points, fingertips touching, palms up, palms down, a fist in the palm, all done with some discretion and restraint. Or, as we mentioned in the last chapter, you could keep your hands busy by holding a pen and occasionally switching the pen from one hand to the other.

2. In addition to releasing tension, your hands can also help make you look a lot more natural. You feel more spontaneous, sound more conversational. Curiously, your voice seems to gain confidence and you may even find yourself on a roll. But it's hard to be on a roll if your hands never move from your sides.

Some further points are:

- If you insist on keeping your hands folded behind your back, you may wind up looking a little too much like a bad imitation of the British royal family.
- Arms folded across your chest is a nonverbal signal that you feel vulnerable. You look like you're protecting yourself and would probably rather be some place else.
- Hands raised up to your sternum (heart) with fingers touching is almost priestly.

FEET

If you have to stand at a lectern (and if you've got a prepared text, you most certainly do), then you've also got to position yourself in one place and stay there. Paradoxically, I tell people that rather than stand planted with feet apart, they ought to place their feet fairly close together—6 inches or so.

The reason for this is simple. Most people doing a prepared text get anxious or bored and start shifting their weight back and forth from one foot to another. This is enormously distracting and sends the signal that you're not really committed to, or even involved in, what you're saying. By contrast, if you put your feet close together and try to shift your weight, you'll probably tip over. Plus, you'll get another inch or two in altitude, and sometimes every little bit helps.

But now that you are stuck in one spot, you'll feel trapped unless you have some way to move around a little. The answer is to stay in the exact same place, but to *turn slightly, by small moves of your feet,* to face different parts of the audience (some of the best political and evangelical speakers do this well).

So let your hands keep moving (perhaps alternately touching the lectern—never gripping or tapping the lectern) and let your feet keep moving, too. If you move your feet gracefully, the audience will hardly notice that you are moving at all.

SHALL WE DANCE?

Now let's quickly walk through what happens when you're called up to speak. Listen carefully to the introduction. The person doing the introducing might say something very personal, poignant, or even witty. Sometimes these seemingly offhand remarks just beg for a response—and if you don't respond, you could appear to be not plugged in to what is happening around you. With luck, you will be able to respond with a line that not only spins off the introduction but also makes a business point relative to what you've come to talk about.

But don't push your luck. If you have a prepared text and can't figure out a way to weave in a one-liner without hurting your strong start, forget it. Just go ahead and begin the way you had planned.

If you are carrying your speech with you (if it is not already waiting at the lectern), conceal it as much as possible by wrapping it around your thigh away from the audience. So as you walk to the lectern, you carry the speech close to your leg.

You have already memorized at least the opening line or two, perhaps the first couple of sentences, *so there is no need to look down* once you get to the lectern.

At the lectern, still trying to keep your manuscript hidden, ease the speech onto the lectern. Look at your audience while you're doing this. If you are right-handed, place the body of the speech on the left side, with the top page on the right. Reverse that procedure if you are left-handed. The reason is that with the speech spread you won't have to move the page for at least the first minute or so.

Now position yourself back far enough so you can still touch the lectern, but at the same time have a good angle for your eye to hit the page. If the lectern is adjustable and someone else spoke before you, adjust the lectern so the rear portion is just below your sternum.

Once you begin speaking, you slide the pages over as needed—*never turn them.* Sliding will minimize the perception that you have a prepared text and help give the impression you are speaking from notes or an outline. This, in turn, will reinforce the perception that you are not reading—which can only mean that you know what you are talking about.

After 5 or 10 minutes you might begin to get a little antsy— *but resist the temptation to let it show by rocking or swaying.* (See Chapter 16.) Stay vigilant and alert to what you're saying. Borrow from the actor. Actors *hear their words in their head* before those words come out of their mouths. So use your pauses as you glance down at each new sentence to *listen to the words* in that moment of silence before you actually say them. Do this hundreds of times, and the effect will be that these words are, in fact, your own—even if someone else wrote them for you, or you are giving someone else's speech.

Pause longer after rhetorical questions and key points. Those pauses may seem agonizingly lengthy (remember, the adrenaline has probably been working overtime), but to the audience you will only look natural, thoughtful, conversational, and comfortable with your subject.

When you finish, don't bolt. Stay long enough to keep your eye contact with the audience. If there is applause, simply say "thank you," pause for another moment, and then leave the podium.

Remember never to show the audience your entire prepared text—if you can avoid it. Slip the speech discretely off the lectern and leave it on the shelf underneath, or slide it back to whichever leg is out of sight of the audience as you walk back to your seat.

PREPARED TEXT BASICS

- Eyes *up-down-up*— not *down-up-down.*
- *Don't shoot* 'til you see the whites of their eyes.
- Pause *before* speaking and *after* speaking.
- *Longer pauses* after "credibility" lines and questions.
- Let your *hands* help you do the talking.
- Keep your *feet fairly close together* so you don't sway.
- *Turn your body* to face different parts of the audience.
- Position yourself *away* from the lectern for better angle of eye attack on the page.
- *Slide* pages, don't flip them.

I should add this important note of caution: Learning to give a prepared text speech as if you were just speaking extemporaneously requires lots of practice. As a rule, I spend only two or three sessions on this skill with corporate people. But with politicians, the work sessions can number five or six—because their jobs depend on being able to use one prepared text after another and *never* appear to be reading.

In a later chapter I will talk about self-training. But the rule for prepared text is simple:

> If you practice at home in front of a mirror and can't see your eyes you're doing something wrong.

The most common arena for prepared text is the big presentation, the big (or important) audience, and the big slide show that goes with it. In fact, most prepared text speeches involve visual aids of one kind or another.

And that will shortly lead us to a very slippery place indeed—the sometimes wacky world of overheads and slides.

CHAPTER
T W E N T Y - T W O

WHEN TO USE
VISUAL AIDS

Overheads, slides, and computer-generated displays are probably the most overused and misunderstood aspect of communications in business. They are almost universally used incorrectly, at an annual cost in dollars and productivity that is hard to imagine. To understand why so often they don't work the way we want them to, we've got to look at the historical big picture.

Visual aids were born as a necessary management tool in the early twentieth century when frustrated senior corporate officers had to devise a way to understand what their subordinates were trying to tell them. Apparently most presentations were as ineffective then as they are today—so senior people decided that if they couldn't get the message from listening, why not try reading and looking at pictures and graphs? That way, they might be able to digest at least a few key points. An added bonus, they reasoned, would be to enforce some kind of quality control and consistency on an otherwise unmanageable mess.

So word slides became part of common business practice, along with schematics, graphs, illustrations, and even photographs. All of which made a great deal of sense. The senior people got the message. They got some measure of consistency. They could even get the presentation in advance if they wanted it.

But they also started something they couldn't stop. Slides and overheads began to grow like crazy. People started to get swallowed up by their visuals. Word slides proliferated. Bullets were everywhere. Presenters came to believe that if they didn't have wall-to-wall visuals they didn't have a credible presentation. Once everybody jumped on the visual aids bandwagon, they were afraid they might look unprofessional if their pitches didn't have as many word slides, for example, as the next guy. Like the arms race, slides and overheads mushroomed until visual aids became an industry unto itself.

As the role of the visuals increased, the role of the presenter decreased—until finally the person doing the talking might as well have sent a substitute or mailed a memo.

In the end, people found themselves simply reading off a wall. Whatever characteristics of leadership or speaking talent they might have brought to the party were pretty much lost. And every time that happens, another opportunity is lost (unless it is your intention to draw attention from yourself and seek shelter behind your presentation, which is a choice a lot of people actually prefer).

> **Visual aids often dominate presentations at the expense of the presenter.**

Today visuals dominate presentations at the expense of the presenter. In most cases, the only reason the presenter has to be at the presentation, personally, is to answer questions.

The fact is that anyone can give a presentation using visual aids. It's easy—all you have to do is to be able to see what's on the screen and be able to read or talk about what you see. The price is that the person doing the talking will probably remain faceless and ineffective—as will the presentation.

EIGHT THINGS NEVER TO DO

I sat in on a meeting recently that seemed to embody most of the problems that occur in the average presentation. The speaker arrived with a huge armload of almost 100 transparencies (overheads) which he dumped in a big pile on a table in the front of the room. You could almost hear the groans as people realized that they were in for a long, and quite possibly, unpleasant experience.

As it turned out, the presentation—and the presenter—more than met their expectations. To begin with, the unspoken message—the hidden agenda—when the manager in question entered the room with his small mountain of visuals was all wrong. The message was, *I'm covering my own backside here, leaving no stone unturned, touching on every possible detail, and if you don't like it or have something else to do, that's too bad. . . .*

That patent arrogance set the stage. What followed further soured the situation:

1 *The lights were turned way down,* shrouding the room in darkness—save for the light from the overhead machine—and nudging people already on the edge of dreary anticipation to retreat into the shadows of frustration.

2 *The speaker turned on the machine immediately* and sank out of sight as the overheads lit up the screen behind him. From the beginning he simply read from, and monitored, his own overheads. After 5 minutes—and before he had even put a dent in the pile—people were already eyeing the exits and checking their watches. A few lucky ones close to doors actually managed to escape (lesson in life: always sit close to an exit).

3 *Most of the overheads were word transparencies*—one word slide after another after another. And the speaker made sure he read every word, including even unnecessary

title and agenda transparencies. Because the audience was able to read much faster than he was able to talk, the frustration built further after just the first couple of overheads. Worse, half the audience was unable to read the small letters on the screen. After 10 numbing minutes, those of us still left had a terrible sinking feeling that we were trapped in a bad situation that we could see was only going to get worse.

4 *The overheads themselves dominated the presentation,* reducing the speaker to the status of a kind of steward hovering in the background. Whatever the steward said soon became no more than just a droning sound. We quite literally stopped hearing what he was saying. Again, you might ask, why is this guy here at all?

5 *There was never a time when the speaker talked without an overhead,* so we never once had a chance to listen exclusively and without visual distraction to what the speaker had to say.

6 *The presentation ran a stupefying 2 hours and 20 minutes.* It is probably fair to say that a good 2 hours of that was an exercise in futility that accomplished little, if anything—when measured against commonsense benchmarks such as clear objectives, enhanced productivity, and good time management.

7 To compound the obvious problem of bad visuals, *the speaker in this case seemed to have no clear message, nor convincing evidence to back up what he did say.* The effect, for all the overheads, was dull, gray, foggy, and flat.

8 Worse, *virtually all the visuals he did use were either the wrong ones or designed incorrectly or used improperly.* Overall, a real mish-mash that did more harm than good. In the end, it would have been better had he used no visuals at all.

I remember coming out of that moribund meeting feeling like someone had injected me with a controlled substance. It was not unlike the distinctly claustrophobic feeling I had once after being trapped for hours in a stuck elevator. It turned out that several others in the meeting had actually succumbed. They had to be awakened when it was finally over.

By any measurement, this is not a good use of our time—and yet it happens in greater or larger degrees in our corporations thousands of times every day. But these crimes against productivity extend even to the corporate off-site meetings and professional conventions where people supposedly go to learn something (again, what we find is that most of what people say they learn they actually pick up chatting and networking *outside* the meetings themselves).

THE EXPERT WHO DIED—AND DIDN'T KNOW IT

I attended one corporate conference which featured a consultant from the Stanford Research Institute who was supposed to talk about business trends in the next century. To protect his identity, I will call him Lars. Lars was scheduled to speak right after lunch—a dangerously soporific time in any event, because a chemical side effect of the process of digestion naturally tends to make us a little drowsy.

Three hundred people were gathered in a large conference hall, all well fed and inclined to doze off. So, in walks Lars and turns off all the lights. Now we are in near total darkness. Right away, half the people in the room can hardly keep their eyes open. On goes the slide projector in the center aisle and now we hear a loud buzzing. Lars never notices it, but within moments there is yet even more buzzing as the sounds of people snoring blend with the noise of the machine like a kind of eerie echo of an ancient temple mantra.

His is not a particularly auspicious start—but Lars is already plunging ahead up on the stage. He's got a bunch of slides which look like maps, organizational charts, complex mathematical tables, and financial statements all overlapping and merged together, one after another in a nightmarish jumble of hyper-data run amuck. To make it worse, the lettering, numbers, arrows, grids, formulas, tables, bar charts, and all the rest are impossible to decipher, let alone read, even in the front row. Not one slide is up long enough for anything other than a squinty glance—bang, bang, bang—and now Lars is pacing around *in the light,* with numbers and lines and arrows like the branches of trees crawling all over his face and body. It's like a Fellini movie, or an outtake from the cult classic *Rocky Horror Picture Show.* Most of the people in the audience who are still awake can hardly believe their eyes. The stagecraft is riveting. Someone later says it was like watching a bad dream. The take-away is zero, but in a sense Lars is so bad he's good.

At this point, the only person in the auditorium who thinks things are going well is Lars. If you listen carefully, you can hear him making dozens of unconnected assumptions as he struts back and forth through the wild jumble of information, his shadow wildly aping his every move on the screen like a crazy mime. But you also begin to become aware of an impression that what he is saying is not necessarily connected to any particular idea and that he is hopelessly out of sync with the madhouse of visual information that keeps dancing all over his face.

After he is finished, none of us had the slightest clue to what he said or even what he was trying to say. Some people applauded, but I suspect that was only because it was finally over. Others may have clapped because they want to be polite. Still others may have felt that anything they didn't understand deserves their admiration.

In any case, you could almost feel the whole room heave a sigh of relief.

Later Lars—knowing I was in the business of helping people sharpen their presentations—had the temerity to ask me how I thought he had done. It was an effort to summon the right words. Finally, I told him, "Lars, that was one of the most astonishing performances I have ever seen." He smiled, and told me he had given that speech a couple of times. He had been fine-tuning it, he said, and added—I suppose in case I didn't get it—that he was considered an accomplished presenter. I could only nod, assuring him that it was a presentation I would never forget.

Later I heard he had been fired from S.R.I. and had subsequently taken a job with a think tank in Washington, D.C. While he's thinking, I hope Lars thinks a bit about how to translate what he's saying so other people can understand.

Lars' story is not uncommon. Every day people take up our time trying to tell us things that we don't get. And a centerpiece of that unfortunate situation happens to be slides and overheads (and more recently, computer-generated displays on TV monitors). Lars unwittingly turned the whole thing into something of a joke, but in the end all the lost productivity that arises out of a poor use of slides, overheads, or monitors is anything but funny.

The irony is that we inflict these wounds on ourselves— and will probably keep right on bloodying ourselves until we change our attitudes and find a better way.

THE CORRECT USE
OF SLIDES AND
OVERHEADS

I think I have found a better way. But before I detail the execution, let me first lay down a few basic guidelines to make it easier (I will refer to slides, overheads, and computerized graphics simply as slides):

1. *Do not begin or end your presentation with slides.* If you agree with the principles outlined in the POWER formula discussed earlier, then you will want to start and end strongly. That means you will begin with one or more of the eight ways to begin effectively and one or more of the ways to end effectively. If you begin and end strongly, you do not need visuals. In fact, slides occurring simultaneously with a strong start or ending are counterproductive. They only serve to distract. If you use slides at all, lump them in the middle.

Exception: Sometimes for dramatic effect you might want to use a group of slides together before you even begin—a fast-moving cluster, say, of new products flashing across the screen, or pictures of the new corporate headquarters, or images that introduce a theme (such as sailboats racing against the wind or sky divers and mountain climbers conquering the heavens and the mountains). This kind of imagery sometimes works best with music.

Or you might want to forget about slides and try a brief videotape with music for even greater impact. One of my clients opened an annual meeting of large corporate sales and marketing divisions by showing a Ferrari—engine screaming—coming straight at the audience, then disappearing at high speed in a roar and a cloud of dust. The imagery was dazzling and set the stage for a fast-moving presentation. The message: Things are changing quickly—and we've all got to learn to win at ever higher speeds. The added value of this very visual approach was that my client's presentation, my client, and my client's message all stood out from the run-of-the-mill presentations that took place over the 3-day conference period.

2. *Isolate every slide by placing blanks or royal blue (or black) matte slides on either side so that the images do not appear back-to-back, one after another.* (I will explain this in more detail shortly.) *Exception:* If a series of several slides is sequential (for example, a build or progression showing a trend) and actually serves to make just one point, then treat that sequence as one slide. This means put blanks on either side of the sequence. Another *exception:* If it is too much trouble to isolate slides and you choose, for any number of different reasons, to run them back-to-back (more on that shortly) make sure to keep them together in the middle of your presentation).

The purpose for isolating every slide is to allow the speaker to dominate—rather than be dominated by—his own slides. Most speakers are unknowingly diminished by their presentations for precisely this reason.

3. *Do not use word slides.* In my experience a majority of presentations rely too much on word slides, so I can guess that this point, especially, will meet with loud objections. But the fact is that word slides usually add nothing. People argue that word slides create reinforcement and double effectiveness.

But the truth is that they provide only redundancy and slash effectiveness.

Word slides that serve the least purpose are titles, agendas, and slides made up of whole sentences and paragraphs. Even bullets are unnecessary—as long as your presentation is designed properly.

It is true, however, that the larger the room, the more legitimate the argument for word slides. As the speaker is reduced in proportion to the size of the auditorium, the greater the need for simple word slides—no more than bullets (key words)—because a sizable portion of the audience may not be able to see the presenter anyway. (But if the speaker is televised on a large screen that dominates the stage, we are back to no word slides.) So with a large audience the word slide does a lot less damage than with a more intimate audience.

Anyone who has ever sat through a business meeting has probably suffered a thousand deaths while the presenter put up word slide after word slide, then dutifully read every single word on every single slide. Nothing could be more frustrating—because most of us can read a lot faster than the presenter can talk. We race through the ten sentences and wait as the speaker is still plodding through the third sentence. Worse, how many times have we been faced with endless word slides—only to find that we can't even read the words because the letters are too small?

On top of that, it is not unusual for speakers to turn their backs on their audiences while they read. This may be the biggest offense of all.

Occasionally, it actually does make sense to use a word slide. For example:

- *Lists.* If you are talking about people, products, or services, and you can't—or won't—use photographs, then it is more efficient to show all the items together. For example, suppose you highlight certain services or products but want to make the point that the services or products are only part of a much bigger picture. You mention a couple of key products, then ask your audience to have a look at all the others. If you have 20 or 30 more products, then they appear chronologically or alphabetically as words in perhaps two columns.

- *Excerpts and quotations.* To support a point, you may want to show a blow-up of a news clip or maybe an excerpt from the annual report or even a quotation from the Bible that makes a business point, or the quotation of a famous person.

As a bonus, by getting rid of most of your word slides you have also probably cut down on the time you will need to give the presentation.

> By all means, keep your word slides in hardcopy form for later handout *after* your presentation, or for your own notes, but *do not* show them to your audience in the form of overheads, slides, or computer-generated displays.

One of the most annoying behaviors people tell me they don't like is when speakers coyly shroud most of a word overhead with a piece of paper, then move slowly down the overhead, revealing one point at a time for what seems like an eternity. The problem here is that this move is too manipulative, because we all know that at this rate it's going to take forever to get all the way down the page.

Another little device that people don't much seem to like is using a pen or pencil or your finger to point to items on overheads. The magnification is so huge that the shadow of the pointer seems to jump spastically and often imprecisely all over the screen. Finger shadows often look fat, sluggish, imprecise, and bumbling. You can lay a pen or pointer on the light tray, and leave it there, but even that is unnecessary—as long as you *tell the audience where to look, then make sure that what they are supposed to look at is highlighted in advance.*

Laser pens—those little tubes that shoot a red dot of light on the screen—are equally awkward. Even if you have a steady hand, the dot bounces around like Tinkerbelle. More about pointers shortly.

Bracketing, boxing, bold-facing or circling, underlining, coloring or otherwise highlighting a number or word is a good idea, because it will help people see at a glance what you want them to see.

Say you have a complex slide full of data, maybe 100 numbers, and for different reasons you are not going to redesign this slide. You know ahead of time that this slide is providing evidence for a particular point you are making, linked, in turn, to a theme. You know that all those numbers are not essential to the point, so you pick the one, two, or three on a P&L statement, for example, that count the most and make sure they stand out from all the others.

When it comes time to show the slide, productivity and retention will also go up—productivity because the audience will focus on the big picture and not have to spend time searching while you are talking; and retention because one or two numbers are a lot easier to remember than 102.

4. *Keep the visuals simple—make just one point per slide.* It is always better to present a simple slide that makes one point, rather than the more common approach of a complex slide that tries to make many points. A complex slide can, in most cases, be reduced to several separate images.

Some presenters try to jam as much information as possible on a given slide, in the mistaken impression that they are being economical and efficient and doing the audience a favor. Wrong. What they are doing, unwittingly, is making the information transfer process a lot harder than it has to be—because what does it profit us to use fewer slides with more data when the audience doesn't get it?

Putting too much on a slide is counterproductive in a number of ways:

- The more information, the smaller the numbers and letters, and the more difficult they are to read.

- The more information, the larger the distraction from what you are saying and the more likely the audience will be out of sync with what you are saying.

- The more information, the bigger the chance for confusion and questions which lead to frustration.

- The more information, the more likely that you are staying away from the central theme and telling the audience more—maybe a lot more—than they have to know.

Exception: Sometimes design engineers by necessity have to show complex schematics—the design of a jet engine or a complicated electrical blueprint, for example. This is fine, because at some point the audience is going to want to know what the whole thing looks like, anyway. But this is not to say that engineers should not make every effort to design simple slides, just like the rest of us. Perhaps *especially* engineers. Some people think engineers often try to build us a clock when all we want is the time.

So as a general rule, the simpler the slide the better. It really is sometimes true that one picture is worth a thousand words. And a simple picture that says a lot is worth a thousand times more than a complicated picture that winds up saying nothing.

Sometimes, however, it makes sense to use a very busy slide crammed with data:

- If you deliberately want to obfuscate, rather than clarify (for example, if the news is bad and you feel obliged not to tell all)

- If you want to impress your audience with the complexity of the issue, enormity of the available information, or outright silliness of a government or bureaucratic process

- If you want to make the point that your recommendations and conclusions derive from deep and thorough research

5. *Use only graphics or illustrations.* If most word slides are out, then what's left is images. The graphics you pick should perform a very simple function. They should help fulfill the W or "window" requirements in the POWER formula. That is, they should provide graphic proof or evidence to back up the central point you are trying to make. Word slides don't do that, so don't use word slides. Graphics do.

Too much light, small monitors, and poor picture quality on larger screens can cut the effectiveness of computer displays.

6. *Make every slide count.* To know which slides, if any, you should use, you need ask only one question: Does this picture reveal a business change? Put another way: Does this picture reflect a new situation, a prevailing condition, a plausible projection? And are those changes, conditions, situations, and projections properly represented by the graphics? Do these graphics connect properly with the main message?

7. *Stick to the basics.* Old-fashioned trend lines, bar charts, step charts, and pie charts will always serve you well. Desktop computer technology and software can produce attractive, colorful, uncluttered slides and overheads at fairly low cost. Some give a nice two-dimensional and three-dimensional effect. If you want to be extravagant and dazzle, you can buy expensive software or hire a production firm to create sophisticated moving graphics that are really moving pictures. These are eye-popping and fun, but they can rivet the audience's attention at your expense and the expense of what you are saying (not to mention the added dollar expense). Like pound cake, these effects are delicious but should be enjoyed only in small amounts.

It should be noted that computer-generated graphics do not, in the main, transfer well to larger screens. They seem to work best in conference rooms or classrooms with monitor screens up to about 48 inches. Old-fashioned slides can still offer the best resolution on larger screens.

Computer graphics work best when the monitor is small (for good definition). But small monitors are unsuitable for all but the smallest audiences. Monitors are also not a good choice when there is too much light in the room (because the image will fade). And image quality, especially on larger screens, can be poor.

Good graphics people understand color and will rarely steer you wrong. Black or a nice royal blue seem to be the most aesthetically pleasing backdrop colors, with green, red, yellow, white, orange, and sometimes purple (sparingly) the other colors of choice. Avoid pastel colors (pale blue, pink, violet, rose, mauve), because they look cheap on a big screen and suggest bad taste. You don't want that perception transferring to the rest of your presentation.

8. *Use one image for one concept.*   If you want to show, for example, a graphic contrasting two years in which your market share went up, the conventional way to do that is to show two pie charts side by side. This works, but not as well as showing, separately, first the one year, then the other. The advantages of isolating the two are:

- The image is now at least twice as big on the screen, which means it is much easier to read and grasp at a glance.

- The concept stands alone, forcing us to focus on one year at a time, and giving us a choice to study some of the other wedges in the pie and how they relate to the big picture.

- When the second image comes up, the contrast is even more impressive, giving us that extra beat to reflect on the striking difference between the two.

9. *Make sure the size of your graphic accurately reflects any change in your company's size.*   This is a neat trick that almost no one thinks of, so you think of it. Say, for example, that seven years ago, your company took in 28 percent of its revenues from its international food business. Then say that today the percentage of revenues from the international food business had grown to 47 percent. But let's say also that in the meantime your company had acquired two other consumer products companies and was now three times as big as it was just seven years ago. To dramatize this change in size, your contrasting, or second slide, would appear roughly three times as big as the first slide.

So the contrasting slides show not only the revenue change but also the size change. This perspective is an important aspect that otherwise might go unnoticed and an opportunity that we often overlook. It can add a dimension that most presentations simply do not have.

10. *Use graphics to depict good news, tables for not-so-good news.* This admonition speaks for itself.

Graphics are, by comparison, a lot easier to understand than tables, which are only graphics in raw data form—in a sense the chaos from which graphics eventually emerge. So it only follows that if you show a graphic you can expect people to quickly understand the point. By contrast, a table is usually sets of numbers often arranged in columns and is far and away a more difficult exercise in comprehension. A table with complex data *confounds,* whereas a graphic of the same information *clarifies.* It is true that a graphic design lurks behind every table, so it should not be difficult to turn a table into a graph, or a graph into a table.

Exception: Many financial people—analysts and others—love tables and often don't even want to hear about graphics. The reason continues to elude me. So in certain financial presentations (analyst presentations included) the visual vehicle of choice may continue to be tables. If that is so, then whatever seems to work best is fine as long as what works best works best for presenter and audience alike (a financial audience, for example, might be able to handle a lot of tables, but any other audience would be better off with graphics).

	YEAR ENDED DECEMBER 31, (IN THOUSANDS, EXCEPT PER SHARE DATA)				
	1995	1996	1997	1998	1999
Statement of operations data					
New revenues					
Widget	$3,016	$5,834	$9,999	$12,720	$14,821
Knick-knack	4	1,302	1,836	2,960	5,815
Other	—	150	112	676	664
Total net revenues	3,020	7,286	11,947	16,356	20,800
Gross profit	1,734	4,664	7,864	10,288	1,351
Expenses					
Selling	1,933	2,618	3,364	4,008	4,958
Marketing	151	87	246	1,035	1,433
Research and development	657	493	966	1,667	1,899
General and administrative	1,535	1,331	2,129	2,518	3,171
Total expenses	4,276	4,529	6,705	9,228	11,461
Income (loss) before international operating expenses, net	(2,542)	135	1,159	1,060	1,890
International operating expenses, net (1)	—	181	460	464	943
Net interest income (expense)	(114)	57	57	(12)	85
Provision for income taxes (2)	—	—	6	30	24
Net income (loss)	$(2,656)	$11	$750	$554	$1,008
Net income (loss) per share	$(1.24)	$—	$.20	$.14	$.25
Weighted average shares outstanding	2,148	3,514	3,707	3,906	4,095

11. *Eliminate all clutter.* I'm talking about even the headline, or the title above the graphic and the occasional cascades of bullets, explanatory notes, or take-away lines at the bottom. Take as many words as possible off the slide until the graphic stands alone, virtually unadorned. Now you have more room to increase the size of the graphic so that it can fill the entire screen. This sheer size and lack of clutter makes an impressive statement. But you have to be careful, as I will note shortly, to make certain that your introduction to the slide and your "roll out" coming off the slide provide all the information that you have eliminated. More on that later.

12. *Limit numbers on any slide to three, if possible.*

13. *Remove the "north" and "east" sides of a bordered slide to enlarge the graphic and focus attention on the concept.* (The more radical among us would remove even the "south" and "west" borders, as well—creating a stand-alone image. This would be my personal choice—it is the only logical conclusion to the proposition that simplest is best.)

A standard statement-of-operations slide in a business presentation might look something like the accompanying table (see page 146).

This might be satisfactory for an accountant or financial manager who is used to working with tables. But for a nonfinancial audience interested only in total net revenues, we may want to redesign a portion of that table to look more like this:

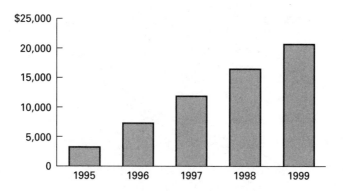

Remove all borders and a few numbers and you get this:

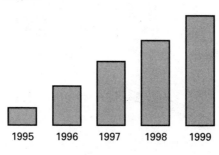

Break down to a simple line chart and you get this:

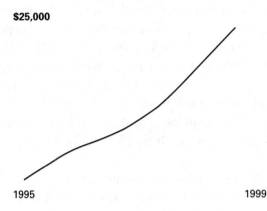

Beef up the line chart so everyone can see it—even 50 rows back:

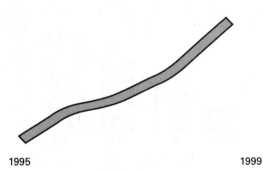

Now throw everything but the graphic away, and you finally wind up with this:

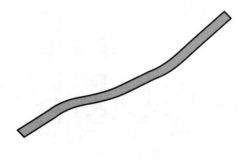

Few people ever actually dare go this far—for fear of looking jarringly different in comparison with their peers. And that is understandable. But those who have tried, at least in my experience, have been applauded, not condemned, for the freshness, clarity, and novelty of their unique approach.

Going back to the statement-of-operations slide, you might show net income this way:

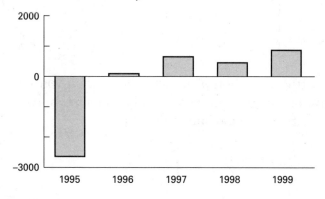

Or like this:

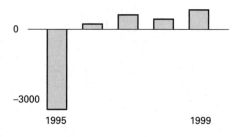

Or this:

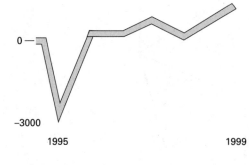

A change in market share is usually depicted in this way:

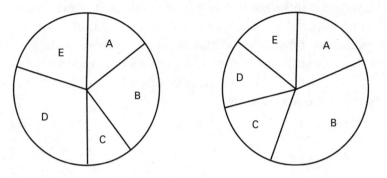

But a true reflection of market share when you measure that share in a larger market should be depicted in two separate pie charts which look more like this:

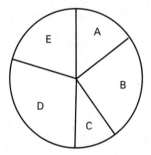

Which would then be contrasted with the larger market—a larger pie—which ends up looking like this:

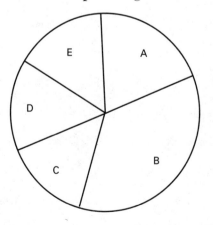

In each case, simplicity and focus seem to leap out at us. The information is condensed into the starkest possible terms, then catapulted into our minds as images that act as snapshots of concept. Weeks later we may still remember the nearly naked graph, whereas a complex table would have long ago vanished into the vapors.

14. If the news is good, or at least encouraging, you might try using fat arrows instead of skinny trend lines to emphasize growth, higher revenues, increased profits, market share or what have you. Then, instead of this:

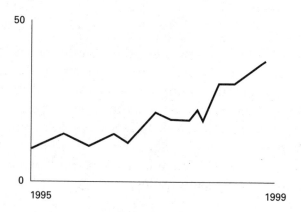

You could show something like this:

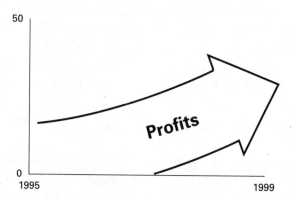

(Caution: Don't even think of using this kind of sweeping trend design if your audience expects real attention to every detail.)

Or even this:

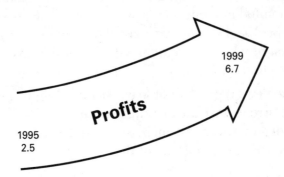

No one will fault you for using the conventional trend line approach, and I do not have strong feelings on the matter. But arrows—especially in presentations involving larger audiences—bring good responses. That in itself might be reason enough to try them. But you should seek the advice and talents of a fairly good graphics designer to figure out when it is appropriate to use arrows in your presentation and how exactly to use them to translate your business message.

15. *Never hand out copies of your presentation in advance.* Naturally, sometimes we have no choice. Corporate protocol frequently requires copies of senior management presentations, board presentations, or analyst presentations to be distributed in advance. For top managers who may miss the actual presentation itself, or need time to review specifics, early distribution can, in fact, be helpful. And some meetings insist on handouts in advance so that participants can take notes.

But for most presentations, handing out copies before or during the presentation is a mistake, because it gives the audience a good excuse not to listen or pay attention. The time to hand out copies of your presentation is *after* it is over.

What you hand out should not necessarily reflect every-thing that was covered in the spoken presentation. For exam-ple, you may have removed all the word slides in your presentation, but you might want to retain the hard copy, or a condensed version thereof, as your notes (*this would include the word slides that you would not show during your talk*). You may also want to include the retained hard copy in the handout version, which may also have more visual and written material that you simply did not have time to cover or chose not to cover in the presentation and Q&A.

> This means, then, that you may actually wind up with two presentations—the one you show them while you're speaking, and the other version.

The other version should be the complete text of what you say (not necessarily what you show) that the people can take home with them.

> Given the opportunity and the time, your clear choice should always be to prepare a slide presentation which shows only graphics, and a separate handout copy that shows everything—graphics *and* word slides alike.

If you have a presentation which you give seated at a con-ference table, and your listeners are also seated, and you choose to use presentation "books," then you have two choices: (*a*) Present with a slim book using graphics only—and after-ward hand out a much thicker, complete version; (*b*) Present with the thicker, complete version, but ask your listeners to refer only to the graphics pages.

OVERHEADS AND SLIDES DO'S & DON'T'S

Don't	*Do*
1. Turn the lights way down.	Let yourself be seen.
2. Turn the projector or computer display on right away.	Establish yourself and your message first.
3. Use word slides.	Stick to graphics, illustrations, schematics, and photos.
4. Allow the presentation to dominate the presenter.	Take charge (see Chapter 24).
5. Flood the presentation with visuals.	Begin and end with no slides.
6. Take a long time.	Keep it as short as possible.
7. Be mushy.	Have a clear message.
8. Use hard-to-read or complex visuals.	Keep the visuals simple (and use only one image/idea at a time).
9. Stand in the light of the projector.	Use a pointer or tell them where to look.
10. Turn your back on the audience.	Keep looking at your audience.
11. Use tables to show good news.	Use graphics.
12. Use graphics to show bad news.	Use tables.
13. Talk about more than one point per slide.	Weave your one theme into each slide.
14. Use laser lights.	Use pointers or nothing.

CHAPTER
TWENTY-FOUR

GOING BY THE BOOK: HOW TO MAKE A STRONG BOOK PRESENTATION

A managing director of a Wall Street firm watched in horror as a presentation that could have been a piece of cake crumbled to pieces in the hands of a brilliant new hire fresh out of Harvard Business School.

At stake were fees of some $30 million. The investment bankers were in the final round of a hard-fought "bake-off" to determine which firm would handle a large merger and acquisition.

Another investment bank was still in the running, so while hopes were high, the outcome was still anything but certain.

The M.D. led the presentation. Everything was going smoothly. He had a good feeling it was going to be all right. In a moment, he would ask this incredibly bright young man with superior math and analytical skills to explain a particular portion of the pitch that needed technical clarification and explanation. They had discussed the details in advance.

Several minutes into the spiel, the M.D. said, "I've brought Andrew with me today to elaborate on that part of the transaction," and signaled his associate to begin.

Andrew's response was perplexing. He pulled his chair back from the conference table, put his presentation book in his lap, buried his face in the book, and began to read from the written text—verbatim. His eyes never came out of his lap.

Hardly able to believe his eyes, the M.D. frantically tried to make discreet hand gestures indicating that Andrew should come back to the table. Andrew misunderstood the signal to mean he was supposed to go faster. So he began to speak almost as fast as he could read.

Meanwhile, the clients, seated on the other side of the table, could only marvel at this bizarre act. By the time the M.D. finally interrupted his prodigy and took back the presentation, it was too late. In the end, the business—and the $30 million that went with it—wound up in the hands of the competing investment bank.

This real-life story leads me to the subject of presentation books, which often can do more harm than good. In this case a lethal combination of a failure to communicate, bad planning, and poor use of presentation books caused an important deal to go south.

Wall Street firms, especially, look and sound alike, and tend to reinforce that perception with "books" that are similar in design and presentations that are similar in content and delivery. So *any* distinguishing characteristics, frankly, would be helpful.

The quickest way to look and sound different is to restructure the standard "books" presentation, redesign the books themselves, and give people a brand new way to deliver their pitches.

Put these elements together, and the presenter—not the book or even the presentation—becomes the decisive factor in the equation. Even the most junior people can wind up looking, sounding, and acting like leaders.

And that's my point: the people doing the listening in these pitches—typically CFOs, V.P.s of strategic planning and V.P.'s of investment strategy and the like—will tell you that what they are really looking for in a presentation is a feel for the person doing the talking.

Does she seem to know what she's talking about? Does she come across as a leader? Is this someone with whom we can have a long-term working relationship?

Sit through eight or nine very similar presentations and what emerges is not the *content,* interestingly, but the *person.* Human psychology can't abide the flood tide of numbers and concepts washing over the mind. In the end, all that remains—the single distinguishing factor—is the person behind the presentation. Or more correctly, the person *in front of* the presentation.

So what can we do to make the person—you—stand out? The answer is surprisingly simple. Just a few quick fixes can make a big difference.

Let's start with the proposition that the POWER formula should serve as a blueprint for *any* pitch, including a "book" presentation. If you accept the principles of the POWER formula, then you recognize the value of a strong start, one idea, concrete examples to back up that one idea, a conversational style, and a strong ending.

The most important thing to remember here is the *strong start* and the *strong ending.*

RULE 1 *Do not begin or end your presentation using the book. Keep the book closed in the beginning, and end. Open it only in the middle, if at all. Fill the now-empty space at the front and back with a strong start and powerful finish. This will give you a chance to position yourself as a leader.*

The conventional "book" presentation has the presenter opening the book right at the beginning. This is common and conventional but not desirable. *The moment you open the book you've lost your own presentation,* because in a sense you've opened a Pandora's box. You will never be able to control what page they're looking at, what they're actually reading, what numbers they are adding, what schematics catch their eye. By definition, you will become a monitor of your own presentation, a droning sound in the background unable to compete with your own stuff. The eye is so much more powerful than the ear, that given a choice, most people will race ahead to look and read—once you've given them an opportunity to do so.

Probably the most direct way to begin—a way that would certainly establish your credentials as a leader—would be to start with the ending (Rule 3 under P in POWER). In other words, come right out and state your case (caveat: this approach might not be as effective with Japanese or Arab businessmen).

So reverse the wave, then surf down that wave with concrete examples to back up your position.

For example, you might begin: "The future of the banking industry lies in consolidation."

This kind of a start sets you up as a credible person worthy of our attention. Someone worth listening to. Now all you've got to do is prove your case—give concrete examples from history or your own experience to support the notion that the future of banking really is in consolidation and your subsequent recommendations.

You may also throw in a personal story, an anecdote, a rhetorical question before you actually ask people to open their books.

Once the books are open, the cat's out of the bag. So you should be sure the books go a long way to help prove the idea of consolidation. Before you end, ask your audiences to close their books; then get their attention by saying something decisive like, "It all comes down to this . . ."

Then give them a concise wrap up—which may include summing up your key point, looping back to the start, asking them to do something, or a story which says it all.

RULE 2 *Don't use word slides (pages in the book that look like word slides). This includes even bullets.*

You may still use those word pages—keep them as hard copy and include them as part of your handout at the end. But don't ask people to read sentences, phrases, and bullets while you're trying to speak.

> If you want to convince your listeners that you're not in command of your subject, there's no quicker way than to use word slides to guide you through your own presentation.

You may want to make separate notes for your own use to keep you on track when you are discussing the material on the word slides, but not actually showing it.

If word slides are out, that leaves you with graphics, illustrations, or schematics *only*. One graphic (one point) per page, blown up large and in color.

RULE 3 *Introduce your next slide while the book is still open to the "old" slide.*

This is like the "roll-in" in Chap. 17, only you may not have time for a "roll-*out*." In other words, you give a few overview remarks covering a step chart, say, on the existing page, then pause, then start your roll-in (your 8-second drill) to the next slide *before you actually turn the page*.

Don't be coy. Tell them all about what they're about to see. Link your roll-in to your theme (consolidation?) and then give a cue line like, ". . . as you can see on the next page." This simple act in itself will virtually ensure that you will not be seen as letting your presentation govern you, but rather as you governing your presentation. You will appear to be in command of your subject—even if you in fact are not.

What I'm saying is that *you never want a simultaneous event*. The mind can't handle two assignments at the same time. *That's redundancy. You want to stagger the event—to introduce the next page and explain the business point relative to that next page, and tie it all to your message, before you turn to the next page. That's reinforcement.*

RULE 4 *Make two separate presentation books. The first book should be made up of graphics only, for the presentation itself; the other, graphics plus word slides (and anything else you want to throw in) for the handout afterward.*

This is, of course, a radical change from what you're probably used to, and a little more work—but the payoff is more than worth the effort.

Now you may have only 5, 6, or 7 pages in your actual presentation, but perhaps 25 or 30 in your handout. All the pages will be graphics. You will have only one graphic per page (but as many as you like per page on the handout version). Your graphics will be positioned sequentially so they help tell your story in the most logical, most persuasive way.

Ultimately, your presentation will probably be a lot shorter, more focused, and more memorable. That's quality. Bring quality to the table and you get the order.

CHAPTER
TWENTY-FIVE

HOW TO CONTROL YOUR PRESENTATION

As you've seen, every presentation involving visual aids ought to really be two presentations—which means a little more work up front but a world of difference in the final product.

The handout version of your presentation is intended for the eye only. But the version the audience sees on the screen while you are talking is meant for the eye and the ear together. That means that the "show" version—the cleaned-up graphics almost devoid of any visual distraction save the central key point—may look very different from the handout.

Better productivity is the reason. It matters a lot less in the handout whether the graphics are bold, eye-catching, and memorable. After all, no one is trying to talk to us while we're studying the graphics and the rest of the hard copy (which would include all the word slides we didn't actually show the audience). Plus, we can read the handout material at our leisure, so we may have all the time in the world.

Not so with the "show." When you are actually presenting to people, you are very likely on a strict time leash. You've got to tell it to them right the first time and be reasonably certain that they got at least the key points (on the theory that even if you did bungle it a bit, you can't rely on everybody in the audience to take it upon themselves to go back later and read the handout). On top of that, most audiences have a limited tolerance for presentations of any kind, so what they see has got to somehow jump out and grab them. (I'm not talking about being melodramatic or fake. But an imaginative and distinctive illustration can get across a business point as well as any lackluster image, so why not with the one that's easiest to remember?)

I should point out here than the main resistance I confront over simpler, bolder, bigger graphics is the old fear of somehow looking too different. But I come back to my point: Who will fault you for being smarter, quicker, clearer, and the bearer of news that is easier to recall?

Now that we know that what the audience actually sees in the presentation may look different from what they hold in their hands, how do we make it all happen?

This is the part that is radically different from what you typically see. In a standard presentation, you are likely to see presenters use their slides as notes. Almost the moment the next slide goes up, the speaker starts talking about whatever is on that slide, sometimes *to* what is on the slide—speaking *to* the screen, instead of the audience.

That approach is routine, but it is incorrect, because when the speaker talks simultaneously with the visual, several bad things happen: *The more slides, the more the speaker is diminished by his/her own presentation.* If we give people an excuse to look at something, they will look—because the eye is 10 times as powerful as the ear. If we are busy looking at a slide, it is often psychologically impossible to pass a quiz on what the presenter is saying. The speaker becomes a slave to his or her own presentation, unable to speak without the "crutch" of the slide. In most presentations, there is no break or relief in the constant parade of slides, which only further reduces the role of the speaker. Typically, the presenter eventually becomes just a mumbling presence in the background.

> The more you rely on slides, the less likely you will come across as a leader.

Let's agree that one reason people present in person—and don't just send memos, voice mail, or E-mail—is because there is real value in having the presenter there physically. It's a career opportunity for the speaker to demonstrate a command of subject, to interact with peers, subordinates, or superiors. And it's a chance for the audience to get a feel for what kind of a person the speaker is. If this is true, then the way we now handle our presentations is unacceptable.

> The presentation should always be an opportunity rather than an obstacle or chore.

People who speak should be seen and heard. Rather than be beholden to their own slides, they should summon those slides only as needed. In other words, they should clarify without slides, then show the audience a slide only when appropriate to provide evidence, then go back to pressing the theme again without slides—until the next opportunity to show another slide: Slide. No slide. Slide again. In this way, you can control the presentation, rather than simply monitor your own slides.

I'll talk more about how that works. But first, it's time to lay down some ground rules:

1. *The proper execution of slides is possible only if we accept the validity of the POWER formula.* Assuming we will not be beginning or ending with slides, and using no word slides, your presentation will have to have a strong beginning and ending.

2. *Since you will now be speaking without any slides at all for a part of your presentation, you may want to use a royal blue or black matte slide with nothing but blue or black on it, rather than just a blank screen.* Some people feel that the blue is pleasing to the eye, while not distracting, and sets up the anticipation that something visual will follow. The blue would also serve as a consistent backdrop to any subsequent slides you would choose to use (the same may be said for black). So either leave the light off in the beginning and end or use a matte.

3. *Be color consistent.*   Using the blue backdrop, make sure that other colors are consistent to class or category. For example, green may represent your company's market share of a certain product or service. Red may represent your closest competitor, and yellow may represent the industry at large. You would want to make sure your greens, reds, and yellows did not vary from their original designation, whether you are using bar charts, trend lines, or pie charts.

4. *Orient your audience to what they are looking at.*   When you put up a slide with a vertical and horizontal axis, for example, be certain to identify what both represent. Sometimes the "yardsticks" are different from slide to slide. On one, you might show units in the vertical and quarterly increments on the horizontal, and on the next slide the vertical might show dollars and the horizontal (which usually represents time) might show an entire decade. Taking care to identify these coordinates will save time and improve communication, because the audience won't have to search, read, and digest while you're talking. Done correctly, everyone winds up more clearheaded and pulling on the same oar.

5. *Use the fewest possible labels and words.*   Not everything has to be labeled or identified with volume numbers, percentages, or dollar figures. Sometimes just labeling the key product, service, item, or market share is enough. You can have six wedges in a pie, for example, which need no representation. You verbally identify them simply as our nearest competitors. You would want to label only your own company and the very big pie piece that shows the market share or the biggest company in your industry (assuming in this example that you are number two).

THE SLIDE GAME

Almost no one plays the slide game correctly—so if you do, you will automatically stand out from the crowd. We can sum up the philosophy of the conventional slide show as "show and tell." Show people a word slide or a picture and start telling them about it right away. That's what you normally see in everyday presentations.

But I have found that psychologically this conventional approach does not—and cannot—work. What works is to reverse the formula completely. *Instead of "Show and Tell," I say "Tell and Show."* In other words, explain *in advance* the entire business point embodied in the upcoming slide. Then show the slide *as evidence to back up what you're saying.* Talking and showing *simultaneously* is self-defeating and redundant.

Talking *then* showing is the way to go. First the exposition then the certification. This one-two procedure repeated throughout your presentation a number of times allows the audience to listen first (to get the point) then to immediately see the evidence and confirm in their own minds how the evidence satisfies the point. This—and only this—is true reinforcement.

Now let's forge ahead and see how this new technology actually works. We'll begin with the assumption that your redesigned presentation will now no longer begin nor end with visuals. When you come to the center of your presentation where you begin to show slides, you repeat the following procedure with each one:

1. *Give an 8-second drill (remember the 8-second drill?), or a summarization of the business news on each slide that supports your position—without yet actually showing the slide.* What the audience sees at this point is only the matte slide or the blank, unlighted screen. In other words, you tell about the business message in the slide *before you show the slide*. This is the *roll in* (sometimes you will roll in to your next slide while your old slide is still on the screen (see page 171). *For example:* "Up until 1993 the industry grew domestically at about 15% per year. But the industry flattened beginning in 1994, with just a modest growth of about 3 percent, until 1995, when the growth numbers started to head south again, as you can see here . . ."

It is not until you have talked about what is on the slide that you actually let the audience see the slide, which should then clearly reflect all the information you just said. Your theme in this case might be that the domestic market has matured and that the time has come to expand globally.

Just about any presentation you see will not be designed this way. The common practice is to speak about the information in the slide at the very moment you show it. Psychologically, that's a tough and unnecessary added burden to inflict on any audience—yet almost every audience, at least in business, has to put up with this inconvenience. Happily, most people don't know they are putting up with anything—because they've never seen it done any other way. The only indication they have that something is wrong is when later they can't remember what they've just heard.

2. *Draw a clear distinction between you talking and the audience looking at a slide.* To be effective, you must *stop talking* to allow the audience to shift from listening to you to looking at the slide you want them to see. So have a *cue line* handy that makes the unmistakable signal that now it's time to look at some evidence or proof to back up your point about the need to expand globally. *For example:*

"Take a look at this. . . ."

"Here's a picture of what I'm talking about. . . ."

"This is how that breaks down. . . ."

"As you can see here. . . ."

Try *not* to say, "This next slide will show . . ." which does not flow as well, sounds too formal, and is, at least in my opinion, too conventional and heavy-handed.

Some people like to ask a *rhetorical question* to introduce a slide:

"So what does it all mean?"

"Where do we go from here?"

"How does it all break down?"

When you are in command of your presentation, you come across as a leader.

"Why does this matter to us?"

"Is there an answer to all this?"

"Can we expect to see a change?"

After you give your cue, the slide goes up (replacing the matte or blank screen or previous slide), and it's time to be quiet. You've got to shut up in order to let the audience digest what you've just said and relate it to what they're looking at now. This is true reinforcement—and tells the audience that *you* are in charge of your presentation, that the presentation is not governing you. You have introduced evidence to back up your theme, and now they are studying that evidence.

This moment of reinforcement occurs in silence. To the inexperienced speaker, silence is a nightmare. But to the person accustomed to speaking—politicians, lecturers, teachers, trial lawyers—silence really is a potent tool. This particular pause used with slides not only emphasizes the value of the words (first) and graphics (second) *delivered separately,* but also, done consistently, the pause helps the listener absorb and retain more information over the entire length of the presentation. That's good productivity.

And because you are in command of your presentation, you come across as a leader.

3. *Let 2 to 3 seconds pass, then give an overview remark.* Your remark should not go into detail or tell too much but should sum up the essence of what the slide means. *For example:*

> "You can see that we did a lot better in the second quarter this year than the same time last year."
>
> "If we keep going like this, we may be in for some real changes sooner than we thought."
>
> "What this tells us is that globalization has been a successful strategy for all our competitors for the last 15 years."

Keep in mind that you may first have to orient your audience to the coordinates—the vertical and horizontal axis, for instance—if necessary. That is, if the measurements and categories change from slide to slide. If you have to do this, do it first, then proceed. You may elect to use a very "clean" slide with no coordinates or indicators whatsoever, in which case you will still have to explain the graphic in terms of any missing information.

4. *Pause again after your overview remark to let that sink in.* Now the audience has heard you make a business point in support of your message, then show a slide to support your point, then give an overview comment to tie it all together. With this pause, which lasts a couple of seconds, the point is even more deeply rooted. Now you drop the slide and up comes the blue matte again (or if the next slide is not a matte but a graphic, you roll in to the next slide while the current slide is still on the screen).

If you choose not to use a matte slide, make sure you have a carousel machine with an automatic "blank" mechanism in between slides to block light, or you can use a conventional slide machine with plastic slugs, or blanks, in the carousel tray between slides. If you use matte, mechanism, or slug, there is no need to turn the machine on and off.

5. *It's a good idea to give extra value by adding yet another remark which serves as a kind of takeaway line. This is what I call the roll out.* The roll out happens after the slide is down and the matte slide or blank is up (or when the old slide is still up, and before the roll in to the next slide—if you are using two graphics, say, back-to-back). *For example:*

> ". . . But those numbers are only preliminary. When the hard numbers come in later this year, I expect the news to be even better." (This could either be over a matte or over the current slide on the screen—just before you start your roll in to the next.)

> "These changes suggest that our market share will grow by more than a third over the next three years."

> "The lesson to be learned from this information is that if we realize our potential in the next three years—and take advantage of key strategic opportunities—we could be number one in the industry by . . ."

> "This information tells us that to grow our business into a worldwide market we've got to act faster, think smarter, and perform better than our competition in every segment of our business."

6. *After roll out, be sure to steer the conversation along the only road that leads anywhere—the road defined by our business message, or theme. For example:*

> ". . . And that's just only more reason that globalization is a good idea."

> "But this will probably not happen as quickly as it could if we don't seize the global opportunities waiting for us right now."

"Again, what we're seeing here are indicators that we might want to form an alliance that would distribute our products to worldwide markets."

Put it all together and you come up with what I call the *hot dog*. Picture a hot dog. The frankfurter in the middle is the visual itself, the slide. The hot dog roll on top is your roll-in. The bun on the bottom is your roll-out. The mustard on the hot dog is your overview remarks. Think of this hot dog as food for the mind:

Food for the mind

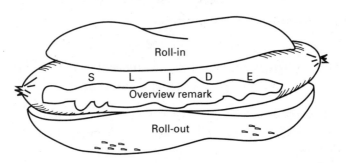

7. *Forge straight ahead with your theme, aiming toward your next slide.* You want to reinforce your theme again and again. Mention it at every appropriate opportunity—which should be often, because if your execution is correct you will be wasting no time or words on anything that does not contribute directly to your theme.

You know you are on track if you can move smoothly from one slide to another, as if they were stepping stones essential to your passage. You're on track if you can comfortably remind the audience of your theme, and your theme is manifested in your slides.

Note: If you cannot or will not isolate each slide with a blank or matte slide, at the very least begin and end your presentation with no slides. In that case, all the slides you use will be clustered in the middle.

> A really clean, well-designed presentation has virtually no waste.

I should also point out here that from a purely practical point of view, and in the reality of the corporate environment, not everybody will feel comfortable exercising these guidelines. For any number of different reasons some people will not separate their slides.

If this is the case, as I have mentioned, *give the roll out while the current slide is still on the screen, then after the roll out, give the roll in to the next slide while the same slide is up. It may not even be necessary to give the roll out, depending on how closely related the slides are.* This way you can create a measure of anticipation, and avoid—at least to some degree—the perception that you are a complete slave to your slides.

A SPECIAL MENTION ABOUT OVERHEADS, FLIP CHARTS, AND CONFERENCE ROOM WALL PRESENTATIONS— AND A FINAL WORD ABOUT VISUAL AIDS

OVERHEADS

What we have said about slides applies across the board in principle to overheads. But the execution may be a little different, because the machine is different. With overheads:

1 *Be certain to use a newer piece of equipment with what I call a "soft button"—often a large red plastic on-off switch—to turn the machine on and off.* Older overhead

machines make a loud clacking noise when you throw the light switch, and the fan sounds like traffic on the freeway. Both distract.

2 *If you prefer a blue matte, you can have one made.*   But you may not like the added chore of taking the matte down and putting it up time and again.

3 *If you are in a conference room, be sure not to stand in the way of those people—often the most senior people—who might be sitting closest to your position near the head of the table.*

4 *Be sure your overheads are lined up correctly on the light tray so they don't wind up looking cockeyed on the screen.*

5 *Use color if possible.*   Color is a lot easier to look at than the conventional black and white overhead. Little X's and meshes and rows of diagonal lines cannot substitute for color.

6 *Make sure all letters, lines and numbers are big enough and thick enough to be read from 30 feet away.*

7 *Don't use word slides. But if you must, don't move down the page showing us one sentence or bullet at a time.*

8 *As with slides, keep your graphic images as simple as possible to reinforce a single point.*   Get rid of title or headlines, bullets, vertical words, numbers, and statistics that are not absolutely bare-bones essential.

9 *Do not use a pen to point to the overhead on the light tray.*   The slightest motion will show up as a bad case of palsy, and pens tend to roll loose even if you let go of them. It's better not to poke around on the light tray at all, but if you must, use a pencil, which will lie flat on one of its planed sides and stay there.

10 *Given a choice, use overheads sparingly.*   Avoid word slides, stick to simple, clear graphics (one idea, one image

at a time). Don't begin or end your presentation with over-heads, and don't try to rush.

11 *Conduct all housekeeping details—taking one transpar-ency off, or putting a new transparency on—in silence.* Don't try to fill the "dead air" with words, because it's enough of a job to get the right transparency on the light tray correctly, without adding the extra burden of trying to talk intelligently at the same time. Remember, the next transparency you put on the tray is not to show immedi-ately, but rather just to be "on deck" for when you need it a moment or two later.

12 *As with slides, give a roll in and a "cue line," pause, push the light switch, pause, give an overview remark, pause, turn off the light switch, give your roll out*, and forge on toward your next overhead.

Overheads may soon go the way of the dinosaurs. They make most sense only in smaller, less formal presentations, where computer-generated displays on monitors are fast be-coming the medium of choice.

FLIP CHARTS

Flip charts can be an asset or a handicap, depending on how you use them. If you decide to use flip charts, follow the same guidelines we have outlined for slides and overhead trans-parencies. In other words, show information *only after you have explained in advance what the audience is about to see.*

This would mean that you would have to prepare your flip charts in advance. Again, avoid using words. What you show should be a graphic, illustration, or schematic. To control the audience's "eye," you would have to *leave every other page blank.* In this way, the conversation comes right back to you after the flip chart has served its purpose. That's what you want. You want the presentation to gravitate back to you as soon as possible.

If you choose to use a flip chart as a work sheet, that's fine. But this usually means writing words as you talk. When flip charts start filling up with words, they become forgettable. Worse, they create an ever-growing distraction that draws the audience like a magnet away from you and what you are saying and toward what you are writing down.

Once you have filled a page, move on to the next.

Some people argue that writing words all over flip charts only aids in the communication by providing reinforcement. I disagree. I think this ploy is nothing more than a facile crutch, providing redundancy rather than true reinforcement. Still, I have seen some very able presenters do a credible job using flip charts. But I attribute their effectiveness to the fact that they are convincing speakers to begin with and not to flip charts. My feeling is that on average they could have done better with no visuals at all. I believe this to be a truth that applies to every good speaker.

A few easy tips to remember with flip charts:

1 *Prepare your flip charts in advance, if possible.*

2 *Use heavy thickness magic markers that make a bold line clearly legible 30 feet away.*

3 *Leave every other page blank.*

4 *Make sure all letters and numbers are at least 2 inches tall.* Leave a separation of at least 3 inches between lines.

5 *Use color—but use it consistently to represent class or category throughout your presentation as you would with slides or overheads.*

6 *Try to write in block, capital letters only (assuming that you feel you must use words).* Block letters are consistent in shape, larger than lowercase lettering, and, if not too crowded together, easiest to read on a flip chart.

7 *Try to write facing the audience.* For some people, this is too difficult. For these people, I would suggest (*a*) keeping writing to a minimum—or prepare flip charts in advance; (*b*) write clearly and quickly when you do have to turn your back on the audience.

CONFERENCE ROOM WALL PRESENTATIONS

The rule here is very simple. If you intend to place your presentation on the walls of a conference room, be certain you reveal only one section at a time as you proceed around the room. This way you will be able to control your audience's attention much better than if they were constantly surrounded on all sides by detailed information. You may need an assistant to cover up the old panels as you move into the new ones. As in slides and overheads, try to tell the story of what's on the next panel before you actually show the panel (again, we are stressing here the very real difference between redundancy and reinforcement. In fact, we are also stressing the difference between yeomanship and leadership).

A FINAL WORD ON VISUAL AIDS

Using this new method we've been talking about does not *always* make sense. The exception to the rule is when companies send out rookies and recent hires to give new business and sales presentations. These are people who do not have a depth of knowledge about their products or companies. Nor do they have a lot of speaking experience. So it is probably a good idea to load them up with trays of slides that can provide some quality control and consistency of presentation and allow them to stay a little more in the background, where they belong. In a case like this, all the "old" rules would apply. (Of course, the real answer to this question is that companies should *never* send very junior people to give any kind of presentation—unless those people have been thoroughly, correctly trained and prepared.)

By contrast, the farther up one goes within organizations, the less desirable it becomes to rely too heavily on visual aids—until you arrive ultimately in the office of the chairman, who should *never* use them.

CHAPTER

TWENTY-SEVEN

AFTER THE SPEECH: THE ART OF Q&A

Ideally, you should be as facile and engaging in your prepared text delivery as you are in your Q&A period afterward. But it's more likely that you will feel more comfortable and judge yourself more competent in Q&A. Since Q&A may in fact be your strongest suit, it only makes sense to strengthen whatever aptitude you already bring to the party. Here are some guidelines I think you should keep in mind.

Be alert—don't relax after the formal speech. Business people are constantly confronted with questions. Some of those questions can be hostile, depending on sensitive or controversial issues in the workplace, prevalence of sexual harassment, equal opportunity, women and minority representation, animal testing, toxic waste, air and water pollution, white-collar crime, for example. So don't get caught off guard. Be prepared—even for the worst. And remember that the Q&A encounter is actually an opportunity to redeem the situation if you feel things have not gone particularly well during the formal presentation.

If you are concerned about getting the ball rolling, station a "plant" in the audience to ask the first question.

Turn any Q&A session with your own agenda. This means that regardless of what you may be asked, come prepared to make several points. You may wish to reinforce what you've already said in your presentation, or to add something that you forgot or didn't have time for, or to hammer home an overriding message. To direct the Q&A session the way you want it to go, use what the media people call "bridging." This simply means answering any question the way you want to answer it. *For example:*

> "Consumer activist groups are complaining that your company is not passing along savings to consumers at the gas pumps from the recent drop in oil prices. How do you answer that charge?"
>
> *Reply:* "I think the real question is, how do you measure real savings after we have spent a year keeping our pump prices artificially low in the face of skyrocketing oil costs?"
>
> "When everyone else was high, we were low. Now the market is fluctuating up and down, but our prices are still relatively low."
>
> "And keep in mind that one out of three dollars we take in goes to oil exploration. That's an investment in our future which will make us self-sufficient—and the only way I know of to guarantee low prices at the gas pump."

This person is obviously prepared. She "bridged" by saying, "I think the real question is" which immediately seized control of the conversation and put the ball in her court. Then she jumped straight to three points she wanted to make.

Caution: "Bridging," if done consistently, is sometimes viewed as evasive. So "bridge" sparingly and wisely, saving the "bridge" only for the hardest questions.

The following are examples of some other "bridges":

"That's much too involved an issue to try to answer in the short time we have here, but what I would like to say is . . ."

"I don't think anyone can give a realistic answer to that question, but what I can say is . . ."

"We've heard that question before, and we'll hear it again, but what we're not hearing is . . ."

"I don't know the answer to that, but what I do know is . . ."

More "bridges":

"The more important question is . . ."

"Sure, that's important. But have you thought about . . ."

"Instead of that, you should ask me about . . ."

I remember the example of the Dow Chemical executive who was asked on national TV about the devastating role of Dow's napalm product in the Vietnam war. The executive replied that while war was tragic, Dow had just developed a vaccine for meningitis in children.

Sometimes you can deflect a pointed question by invoking legal or corporate protocol:

"I'd like to answer your question, but our lawyers have asked me not to just yet, because the matter is still in litigation. . . . What I can say is . . ."

"We'll have to withhold our answer until we've had a chance to review all the facts. . . ."

"We have decided to hold off until senior management has had a chance to look at the facts and agree on an appropriate response. . . ."

"We can't talk about that until we know more—because if we do, we're afraid someone might get hurt."

"Bridging" assumes you have something to bridge to, so arm yourself with a laundry list of points, then take the time to rehearse your answers to tough questions with an associate. *Don't answer too quickly—for three reasons.* A pause before answering: (1) Gives you time to think your answer through before talking. This will likely shorten your response, get rid of those talking-while-thinking "uhs" that are only a way to buy time while you think, and eliminate redundancies. (2) Tells the audience that you are a thoughtful person who doesn't shoot from the hip. (3) Most important, provides a consistent pause in the event you're asked the patently unfair or unexpected question that comes right out of left field. With a consistent pause before all your answers, you won't appear to be reeling when the tough question finally does come. And the people asking questions won't spend the remaining time dwelling on that issue.

Tell the truth. Whatever you do, don't lie—because you'll probably get caught. If you don't know an answer, say so, then offer to provide the answer as soon as possible. Or if the truth hurts, then be prepared in advance to deal with that issue.

Be concise. Try not to over-answer. We're all guilty of talking too much at some time or another. But talking too much in Q&A can be counterproductive. For one thing, most listeners are comfortable with conversational "sound bites" of roughly 18 seconds, and if you talk longer you should have good reason. (If you don't think 18 seconds is a long time, check your watch and count off 18 seconds of silence. It's actually a surprisingly long time.)

If you have thought about questions and answers in advance, there should be little reason to give long answers. Besides, long, rambling answers often signal a poor preparation, fuzz thinking, discomfort, and redundancy.

Get right to the point. This is a point I can't stress enough. A person thinking clearly won't build to an elegant conclusion. Rather, the Q&A master will often jump right to the main point (reversing the wave), then explain briefly how he/she came to that conclusion.

> A good example or two will go a long way to providing credence.

If you do have good examples, don't be shy about busting right through the 18-second "sound bite" to go longer than 18 seconds.

Stay cool. Don't get into a spitting match with a skunk, because you're bound to lose. Stand your ground and be firm if someone is taking shots at you, but also try to be courteous.

Be sincere. Simple sincerity is a winning grace. Humor can be a useful weapon in a hostile interview, but try to avoid coming across as a comedian. Often humor is seen as sarcasm or insensitivity and can backfire.

Beware of false premises. You may get a question that is based on incorrect facts. If so, correct the facts and set the record straight before you go on to answer that question. However, if the questioner uses egregious adjectives such as "howling," "unwise," "stupid," or "incompetent," ignore the provocation and forge ahead with an answer, perhaps a "bridge," that lays bare the lie and turns the situation around.

Don't say "No comment." We hear "no comment" all the time on TV, but these two little words provide a lot more problems than solutions. "No comment" suggests that you are stonewalling—even though you may not be.

I remember the story of the oil company CEO who cautioned his vice president of corporate affairs never to speak to the press without first consulting with the CEO. One day when the CEO was away on a fishing vacation a tank farm blew up, throwing flames hundreds of feet in the air. When the news people showed up the hapless vice president stood in front of the fire saying "no comment" over and over. Of course, he had nothing to hide, but the next day local headlines hinted darkly of a secret nuclear facility or special government top secret weapons program gone bad.

To avoid this unnecessary embarrassment, and still satisfy his CEO, the vice president need only have said something sensible like, "We have a problem and we're working to fix it. As soon as we know more we'll let you know."

When several questions are asked by the same person at the same time, don't feel obliged to answer more than one. Pick the one you like, answer it, then move on. If you wish to answer all the questions, you may have to take a couple of notes, or ask the questioner to repeat his or her remaining questions.

During the course of the Q&A session, don't respond to the same question twice—even if it is worded differently. Say that you have already answered that question and move on.

If, in the beginning, you have no "plant" and no one seems to want to ask the first question, ask yourself a question to get things going.

Don't prolong the Q&A period. When you've got past the prescribed time limit, or sense the meeting has gone on long enough, say something like, "We have time for one more question," answer that question, and then stop.

Tape the session. It's helpful to have a video or audio verbatim transcript—not only so you can see how you did but also if the subject matter is particularly sensitive. It's not a bad idea to have your own record of what you actually said.

CHAPTER
TWENTY-EIGHT

DEALING WITH
THE MEDIA

A recent survey revealed that more than half of all executives polled so distrust TV reporters that they would flatly refuse to be interviewed on television under *any circumstances.* This is understandable, given the rabidly aggressive nature of *Sixty Minutes* and all its subsequent imitators, such as *20/20* and *Hard Copy,* and considering the generally antibusiness bias behind most TV stories involving corporations.

Yet for those who feel they have a story to tell and are willing to view the medium as a stepping stone rather than an obstacle, television is an opportunity almost too good to pass up. Handled properly, one free minute on network TV can be worth more than a year's fees to Madison Avenue.

Here are a few suggestions:

1. *Consider yourself on the air from the moment you walk into the studio.* No need to be paranoid, but keep in mind that careless chatter with an associate about what you *should not be saying* could be overheard by an ambitious production assistant and wind up on the air as an unwelcome interview question.

2. *Care more about the message and the points you want to make than how you are doing.* If you do, you probably won't have to worry about how you are doing, because your commitment and focus will gather momentum and carry the day.

3. *Know your show.* What is the show's format? Controversy? Confrontation? Political? Social? Bizarre? Is the host bright, stupid, angry, ambitious, liberal, conservative? Does he or she prepare thoroughly? Or does the host reveal more style than substance? Knowledge of what you are getting into can give you a better idea of how to conduct yourself.

4. *Think the right thing.* Rather than picture yourself in a defensive posture, take the opposite view and go on the offensive.

See yourself as a prophet of enlightenment. Try to be positive, helpful, enthusiastic. Clarify and instruct. Give vivid examples. Take a genuine interest in trying to convey your answer and/or point of view in the most helpful way you can.

5. *Don't attack your opponent.* That's just bad form—especially when he is not there to defend himself. Feel free to question logic, reasoning, or conclusions, but resist the temptation to impugn one's character or motives. People who stoop to personal attacks can be themselves seen as suspect.

6. *Avoid "secret-handshake" language that smacks of the corporate, bureaucratic, or heavily academic.* It's a "home," not a "domestic habitation unit." It's a "death," not a "hospital care negative outcome." It's a "bond," not a "fixed income vehicle." It's a "doctor," not a "primary health care deliverer."

7. *Listen carefully.* How well you do can depend on how well you listen. If you are on a panel show or a show with a central point of origin and other people at several "remotes," pay attention to *all* the questions and *all* the answers. Be on the alert for "loaded" questions based on false, misleading, or openly hostile premises.

8. *Be yourself.* Need we say more? Don't try to change or act out a role, because you may wind up looking and feeling fake.

9. *If pressed hard, question the questioner.* During a contentious campaign interview in the 1980s, George Bush suddenly counterattacked and started asking pointed questions of Dan Rather on national TV. The tactic clearly caught Rather off balance, and left Bush looking like a victor.

10. *Plan your quotable quotes in advance.* In an interview there's nothing like a clever label or phrase to grab people's imaginations. Churchill coined "iron curtain" and "summit conference." Other familiar standbys are "silent majority," "new deal" and "cold war." You may not see yourself as another Churchill, but you can use evocative standbys such as "ticking time bomb," "accident waiting to happen" to reinforce your case.

11. *Use statistics sparingly and wisely.* Reinforcing your point with statistics adds credibility, but can clutter your message. Stick to no more than two statistics per point, and—as always—keep it simple. For example, "83 percent of people polled said they support the measure, but only 15 percent said they would be willing to pay extra taxes."

12. *Cite your personal experience.* Whenever possible, draw on your own eyewitness recollections. There is no substitute for actually having been there. For example: "People complain about bureaucracy and how they never seem to get anything done. But in the three years I spent in local government, I saw more projects completed than in the previous 20 years spent in a big corporation."

13. *Defuse loaded questions.* Techniques for doing this include: (*a*) disagreeing with the loaded premise ("I don't agree with your characterization of American managers"); (*b*) recognizing that some people may agree with the loaded premise ("It may be true that some people feel the way you do, but . . ."); or (*c*) bridging immediately to your position ("It may be true that some people feel the way you do, but most people fail to consider that . . .").

14. *Don't be afraid to change your mind.* It's okay to change your mind. More than one major reversal in a lifetime is probably too often, but we should feel free to change our minds about issues as the circumstance surrounding those issues change. Robert McNamara, the former Secretary of Defense under Presidents Kennedy and Johnson, and chief architect of America's aggressive military involvement in Vietnam, changed his mind. Years later, McNamara finally admitted he'd been wrong in Vietnam and wrote a book about it. A change of heart can signal flexibility and open-mindedness, so admit when you've changed your mind and be prepared to explain why.

15. *Assume the microphones are always "hot"—even before and after the show, or during commercials.* This means don't say anything you wouldn't be comfortable saying on the air or having immortalized on tape. No one wants to become part of a "blooper" reel.

16. *Try not to nod when interviewers are asking you questions.* You know that your nod is a courteous sign which says, in effect, "Yes, go on, I understand . . ." or "I am listening . . ." But on TV your nod, particularly in conjunction with a hostile or pejorative question, can seem to mean, "I agree with your damning assumptions" or "Yes, I am guilty and ashamed." Feel free to nod only if you happen to be in wholehearted agreement.

17. *Wipe sweat off your brow with your finger, not your handkerchief.* TV lights can sometimes be uncomfortably hot, and it is not uncommon for people to perspire. If you feel beads of sweat developing, try to discreetly run your forefinger along your brow. Should you choose a handkerchief, it would look like it was the question, not the lights, which are making you sweat. Using your finger can actually give the impression that you are thoughtful.

18. *Never play to the camera's little red light.* Instead, keep your eyes on the host or other panelists at all times, and try to imagine that you are having a conversation that approximates a relaxed social situation. The studio director controls the action, so don't waste your time trying to find the "on" camera. You will only wind up looking distracted and untrustworthy. Besides, unless you are a professional on-air "talent," you will appear to be grandstanding.

19. *Never look at yourself in the monitor.* In most studios, the monitor will be hidden from view, but if it is not, resist the temptation to check yourself out and see how you look. You will appear distracted and inane to people watching. Instead, concentrate on the host or panelists, and later request a tape of the show.

20. *Try to be as "likable" as possible.* "Likability" counts for a lot on TV. You can measure likability in several ways: by staying cool and reasoned under a bullying attack; by showing a sense of humor; by being prepared with facts and figures and revealing a genuine desire to enlighten and be helpful. It is conceivable that you could feel you fare badly during the interview, yet wind up actually getting high marks—based on nothing more than how well you came across.

21. *Try to be crisp.* The average on-air news "clip" of people talking is only 18 seconds. That's perhaps 80 words or less. Because of the demands of available air time and deadlines, tape editors will typically favor the shorter cut for later broadcast. Best solution: If you feel you can answer the question without bridging, go straight for the conclusion, with a fact or figure or anecdote to back it up. You may even have some time left over.

CHAPTER
TWENTY-NINE

HANDLING HECKLERS

There is no easy way to defuse hecklers, but you need never be the victim of someone who tries to steal your platform and grandstand at your expense.

Humor can be a potent weapon in the right hands. Former Secretary of State Alexander Haig was speaking at the United Nations when a group of Puerto Rican separatists began shouting at him from the first row of the mezzanine-level spectator's gallery. Without missing a beat, Haig stopped his speech just long enough to say that he was unable to hear what the men were trying to say, but "if you would just step forward a few feet I'm sure I could hear you a lot better." The audience laughed, and the hecklers sat down and stopped heckling.

In a political campaign, any heckling can be an opportunity for the heckled. In the 1980s, while campaigning for election in the Northwest, President Reagan was repeatedly and loudly interrupted by a small group of activist priests. Reagan immediately saw his opening and declared, "This, ladies and gentlemen, is why I'm here—this is democracy in action. The very system that these people are complaining about is the system that makes it possible for them to be here shouting at the President of the United States. And I, for one, intend to protect their rights as long as I'm in office."

Fictional personal attacks are fairly common. Take, for example, the heckler who shouts something like, "When was the last time you cheated on your taxes?" This largely rhetorical question is intended to draw attention to the questioner at the expense of the person being heckled. It is meant to cast by suggestion, a bad light on the morals or character of the speaker, while endowing the heckler with the higher moral ground. But more often the tactic backfires, and the heckler winds up looking like the bad guy.

You might recast that loaded question this way: "The question has come up as to whether I pay my taxes like everybody else. The answer, of course, is yes. Next question . . ."

Or you might want to put a light touch on the situation by taking a stab at humor: "I admit the thought has actually crossed my mind. But my wife tells me I'm a bad liar, so I think I'll leave cheating to those who have a much higher tolerance to gambling and the risks of living dangerously."

The chances of your being heckled in most business or civic speaking situations are not high. But it's always nice to be prepared. The key objectives with hecklers are:

- Be firm.
- Be courteous.
- Control the situation.

Sometimes it's tough to be courteous and hold your ground at the same time. But hecklers have no intention of engaging in rational discourse. Hecklers throw caution to the winds. They bully and grab all they can when they can, leaving most of their targets feeling frustrated and violated and without a clue of how to appropriately respond.

Here are a few simple tips that could help if the going gets tough and someone starts heckling:

1. *Deflect the heckler.* Listen for 5 or 6 seconds, long enough to appear courteous, and until you can be certain you're dealing with a real heckler who does not intend to shut up. Counterattack by firmly interrupting the diatribe in progress. Butt back in by assertively asking the question, "Are you asking me a question or are you making a statement?"

If the heckler responds that he or she is asking a question, then demand the question. Now the control of the conversation rests again with you. The heckler asks a question, and you can respond by (a) dismissing the question with a simple "yes," "no," "of course," "perhaps," or "maybe" and then quickly moving on to the next question; (b) bridging to a point you want to make, or (c) answering the question honestly and sincerely, without elaboration. The idea is to dispose of the question as quickly as possible and to press ahead in another direction.

If the heckler responds that she or he is making a point, you quickly cut in to remind the heckler that the time available will not allow statements—only questions, but that you or a representative would be happy to meet the heckler afterward to discuss the issue further. Then, of course, you should show good faith and make good on that pledge.

If the heckler won't back off and won't stop the disruptive behavior in spite of all your best efforts, then you have no choice but to turn to another part of the audience and ask for another question. Remember, in most cases, you have the microphone. If you don't have a microphone, forge ahead anyway. If there is no other question forthcoming, you can always ask *yourself* a question, such as: "People frequently ask me, What is the toughest part of your job? And my answer often surprises them. My answer is. . . ."

If the heckling continues, you can caution the heckler that if he or she does not sit down and let other people be heard, then you won't even agree to meet afterward. Or you can threaten to have the heckler taken out by security. Or, as a last-ditch defense, you can declare the Q&A session at an end, thank the audience, and leave. (Don't forget to turn off the mike when you go.) This last tactic could be viewed as a victory for the heckler, so it should probably be used only in extreme situations when things are clearly getting out of hand and there seems to be no chance of regaining the floor with dignity. Typically, you would have to be facing more than one very enthusiastic heckler to be forced to take this action.

2. *Rephrase the question.* Sometimes a heckler, when pressed to ask a question, will counter with some heavily biased vitriol so loaded with innuendo that it just begs to be recast as a simple declarative sentence. Not only does rewording the question remove the sting, but recasting makes the question a lot easier to answer.

For example, an angry former employer shows up at a new product launch and shouts: "Why don't you tell them about the pollution your factory is pumping into the town's groundwater every day?"

Your response could be: "The question is . . . what are we doing to improve the environment in our community? The answer is . . . a lot . . . and there's nothing secret about it" (then explain your pollution initiatives).

Happily, heckling is infrequent. The first heckle is always the toughest. If you expect to be a leader in your business or organization, you can expect a little heckling from time to time. You can also expect to surprise the heckler.

TRAINING YOURSELF

Advanced technology, mass production, lowering cost, and the demands of the information age have made it possible for more people than ever before to have access to camcorders (television cameras with built-in tape recorders and playback capability). For people who want to become good speakers, no tool is more handy or more informative.

> People who teach golf, skiing, and tennis have known for years that nothing speeds the learning process like showing someone a tape of themselves trying to perform a test of skills.

The subjects of these revealing tapes study every move and every nuance with uncommon attentiveness, because they are, after all, watching themselves—and they don't always like what they see.

The same is true for the role of the TV camera in helping people (1) see themselves as others see them; (2) spot distracting body movements or gestures; (3) practice for speaking assignments; (4) perfect key elements like pause and eye contact; and (5) monitor their own progress and improvement as they advance through a program like mine to develop their own speaking style.

Even if you have never had even a single minute of professional help or speaker training of any kind, regular use of a camcorder set up with a tripod and TV monitor in your own home or in your office will help make you a more effective talker. The reason is that most people are acutely sensitive to whatever shortcomings may show up on tape. Once you identify the offending elements, it is easy enough to practice until they go away. It is important, though, that you don't see a swan as an ugly duckling and then proceed to kill the swan. So I suggest that if you undertake to practice with a camcorder, you also undertake to apply the principles you learn in this book. You may also wish to identify with your favorite speakers in government, business, or show business. If you think it can help, borrow whatever attributes you see in them to perfect your own speaking game.

However, if you don't trust yourself to get it right (because you're not sure what you're supposed to be looking for—even after reading this book) and if you are really serious, you can always hire someone to help you. For individuals this could be seen as an extravagance. But for a corporate person or someone running for public office, private training is an abundantly rewarding investment that makes good business sense. (Of course, one could argue that people like me are part of the problem and that we may have done our jobs too well— because many of our clients in politics and in business have only added to our fiscal and regulatory woes.)

Finally, I should mention that if you don't have a camcorder, can't afford one, don't want one, or can't rent or borrow one, you can practice with a mirror. Practice the POWER formula. Practice the 8-second drill. Experiment with eye contact and pauses for emphasis.

The golden rule, which I mentioned earlier, bears repeating: If you can't see your eyes—that is, if your eyes are not eye-level the whole time—you're doing something wrong.

CHAPTER
THIRTY-ONE

WHAT'S IT ALL
WORTH TO YOU?

Most people view the process of so-called public speaking with silent distrust. They see it—and rightly so—as a high-risk pursuit fraught with arcane ritual best left to fools and the high priests of the podium.

I, for example, do not have a natural aptitude to inspire, clarify or inform. Given a choice, I would prefer to remain silent, stay out of the limelight, and get on with my business. Yet I do open my mouth and say things—because I know I have to. Any apparent "aptitude" is the result of attitude, hard work, and determination.

Of course, there will always be a remarkable handful that seek—and find—center stage with a burning passion the rest of us will never completely understand. Others rise through life with an ease that astonishes their friends, then find they have a surprising talent with words and a seemingly God-given gift for charming audiences.

But *all* of us, like it or not, will eventually see our reputations, careers, and even our social lives determined to some significant degree by how well we speak. Are we forgettable—or do people remember us and act on what we say? Are we boring—or do we spark interest and get people involved? Do

we hide our intelligence and potential by the way we speak—
or reveal ourselves in the best possible light?

In the big picture we are talking about leadership (leaders
lead with their words), issues management (what to say, when,
and to whom), time management (let's not spend more time
than we have to preparing), productivity (are they getting the
message?), and effectiveness (did we get results—did they do
what we wanted them to do?).

Like it or not, our own words will likely determine our lot
in life. Even how we answer the phone can have an effect on
our future. An inarticulate response in a meeting can sabotage
a whole career. Poor eye contact and mumbling can put an end
to hopes of advancement in any organization.

Is it possible to put a dollar amount on the business value
of good communications skills? I remember when the new
CEO of a company said to me, "You know, this stuff is great,
but I don't know how to measure it. I don't feel like I can get
my arms around it." This CEO came from the finance side of
the business, so he tended to feel uncomfortable without specific yardsticks to mark progress. He was challenging me to
reassure him that the money he was spending on speaker training was a good business investment.

My answer was simple. I told him I did not know, either,
how to render an exact measurement. But I reminded him of
the first time we had worked together, shortly after he had
become CEO. My assignment was to prepare him for his first
series of analysts' meetings. We met three times in two-hour
sessions. The day after the first analysts' meeting, the stock
shot up 4⅝ points, producing a paper profit to the corporation
of a little under $100 million.

So I told him that by any reasonable measurement, if he
credited the work we did together for just one-tenth of 1 percent of that share price increase, my fee was still just incre-
mental by comparison. He could only laugh.

Each of us has it within ourself to shape our own destiny—
and it's an exciting prospect to know not only that there is

always room to grow but that it's actually fun to constantly improve at whatever we do.

When I was a boy, I learned to ski. I still ski. When I was a bit older, I learned to ride a motorcycle. I don't drive a motorcycle anymore, but I could if I had to. The same for tennis, golf, and flying a plane. Once you learn the rules and the moves, you can play the game. The more you play the game, the better you get. The better you get, the more fun you have. The more fun you have, the more likely you are to be successful at whatever you do.

In the United States today, very few people ever learn to play the speaking game. If they do play, they often play by the wrong rules—as we've seen in these chapters. I see a lot of lost opportunity for millions of people struggling to make it in a tough, often unforgiving world. How much easier their jobs would be, I am convinced, if they would but learn to play the game.

Becoming a player can be surprisingly easy. Simply understanding the basics in this book, then applying them, can make a measurable difference *right away.* The payoff is so rewarding and accessible, there can be no logical or reasonable excuse for *not* making a conscious decision to alter our own lives for the better:

For the CEO who wants to be seen as a leader.

For the COO who wants to be CEO.

For the CFO who wants to drive the stock straight up.

For the lawyer who wants to serve her clients better and build her practice.

For the salesman who wants to run his own region.

For the researcher who wants to help his clients and his own management understand the incomprehensible.

For the teacher who longs to inspire his students.

For the entrepreneur who seeks investors to build her business.

And for all the toilers in all the vineyards who ever wanted to leave the world a little better than the way they found it. The payoff I am talking about will work for anyone willing to work for the payoff.

Mediocrity is not an inevitability. The way out of mediocrity is implementation—simply using what you read in this book.

INDEX

ABOUT THE AUTHOR

Granville N. Toogood is a top executive communications expert, as well as an established speaker, trainer, and writer. Prior to starting his own company in 1982, Mr. Toogood was a television reporter and network news producer for NBC and ABC. Today he works with a long list of blue-chip clients and has served as a consultant to 38 of the Fortune 50 CEOs, as well as thousands of senior-level executives, elected officials, and diplomats throughout the world. This book is based on his acclaimed corporate workshops in executive communications. Mr. Toogood resides in Darien, Connecticut.